Heroes and Heroines of the American Revolution

By Robert C. Jones

Robert C. Jones
P.O. Box 1775
Kennesaw, GA 30156

jone442@bellsouth.net
rcjbooks.com

First Edition

ISBN: 1507803826
EAN-13: 978-1507803820

Table of Contents

Introduction

Its been 239 years since the Declaration of Independence was signed. In modern America, many people consider the Founding fathers (and Mothers) to be quaint, distant figures from the past, with little to offer us in the modern era.

However, nothing could be further from the truth. The heroes and heroines of the American Revolution were monumental figures that changed not only America but the world. Some of them were brave on the battlefield (Washington, Daniel Morgan, Francis Marion, Molly Pitcher, Margaret Corbin). Some were brilliant political thinkers, who gave the world a new form of governance (Jefferson, Hamilton, Madison). Some were great patriot writers and orators for the cause (Henry, Warren, Paine). Some of them came from overseas to help the American cause (von Steuben, Lafayette). Some were great diplomats (Franklin, John Adams). Some were spies who risked their lives for the cause, and some of them forfeited their lives (Nathan Hale, Lydia Darragh). And some were revolutionaries who risked their fortunes for the Revolution (John Hancock).

George Washington is among the greatest military leaders of all time. His strategy and execution at Trenton, Princeton, Monmouth and Yorktown are still studied today. Benjamin Franklin was one of the great scientific minds of the 18th century, and probably would have been successful in any endeavor he'd taken on. John Paul Jones is the father of the United States Navy, and Betsy Ross gave us our first flag.

I've selected 32 heroes and heroines for this book (20 men and 12 women). Are there others that could have been added? Of course – John Jay, Aaron Burr, John Dickinson, Henry Knox, Joseph Warren and others – could have been part of this book. But I included the 32 people that I thought had the biggest impact on the American Revolution. They are listed in alphabetic order – I'll make no attempt to rank their importance

As with all of my recent books, as much as possible I allow actual participants in the events described herein to tell their own stories. This is made possible by projects such as Google Books and those of various universities which have made heretofore out of print titles available in a digital format. I've tried to include three quotes either by the person in question themselves, or by a contemporary. In the case where there are no documents by or about a person, I've sometimes quoted from newspaper accounts either from the 18th century, or sometimes from centennial – type articles ("100 years ago today").

Note that I maintain Colonial spelling in quotes from source documents, except in situations where the spelling makes the excerpt difficult to read. Also, as a personal quirk, I prefer to refer to places by their name in the United States of America, even before such an entity existed. Thus, I'll refer to "Connecticut" rather than "Connecticut Colony"

I hope you enjoy this look at *Heroes and Heroines of the American Revolution*

Regards,

Robert C. Jones
Kennesaw, Georgia
February 2015

Heroes of the American Revolution

John Adams

> Facts are stubborn things; and whatever may be our wishes, our inclinations, or the dictates of our passion, they cannot alter the state of facts and evidence. (John Adams)

Date	Events
October 30, 1735	Born in what is now Quincy, Massachusetts
1755	Graduates from Harvard; teaches in Worcester, Massachusetts
1758	Receives law degree from Harvard, and joins the bar
October 25, 1764	Marries Abigail Smith (a third-cousin). They would have 6 children, including John Quincy Adams (b. 1767).
1765	Stamp Act passed (a tax on printed materials).
August 1765	Writes a series of articles for the *Boston Gazette*, opposing the Stamp Act
September 24, 1765	Writes the *Braintree Instructions*, which instructed the Massachusetts legislature representative from Braintree, Massachusetts to oppose the Stamp Act
December 1765	In a speech before the governor, Adams slams the Stamp Act, and announces that the Act is invalid, since Massachusetts Colony has no representation in Parliament
1766	Braintree, Massachusetts elects Adams as their selectman
May 16, 1766	The Stamp Act is repealed, after most tax collectors are pressured into resigning
1767	Townshend Acts passed
1767	John Quincy Adams is born
1768	John and Abigail move to Boston
October 1768	British occupy Boston
March 5, 1770	Boston Massacre. Adams would go on to defend the 8 British soldiers involved. Six were found not guilty, and two convicted of manslaughter.
April 1770	Parliament rescinds the Townshend duties, except the one on tea
June 1770	Elected to the state legislature (Massachusetts General Court)

Date	Events
1774	Intolerable Acts (Coercive Acts) passed against Massachusetts
March 31, 1774	Boston Port Act (part of the Coercive Acts) passed. It was, essentially, a blockade of the Boston port.
September 5, 1774	Member of the First Continental Congress
1775	In *Novanglus; or, A History of the Dispute with America, From Its Origin, in 1754, to the Present Time*, Adams disputes the Parliament's authority over the colonies
May 10, 1775	Member of the Second Continental Congress
June 1775	Nominates George Washington as Commander-in-Chief
April 1776	*Thoughts on Government*, written by Adams and published by Richard Henry Lee, becomes a reference for states developing state constitutions. The document supports a bicameral legislature, republicanism and separation of powers.
1776	Assists Thomas Jefferson in writing the Declaration of Independence, and is active in getting it passed through the Continental Congress (July 4, 1776)
September 11, 1776	Adams and Benjamin Franklin meet with Admiral Richard, Lord Howe on Staten Island in an abortive Peace Conference
1777	Adams becomes head of the Board of War and Ordnance
April 1, 1778, to June 17, 1779	John accepts a diplomatic post in France
1779	Helps draft (with Samuel Adams and James Bowdoin) the Massachusetts Constitution
November 14, 1779	Adams leaves for France for a second diplomatic tour
1780	Becomes a founder and charter member of the American Academy of Arts and Sciences
April 19, 1782	Achieves recognition of the United States as an independent government from the Dutch Republic; during his time in the Netherlands, he also procures a loan of 5,000,000 guilders.
November 30,	Adams signs the peace treaty with Britain

Date	Events
1782	
1784/85	Treaties with Prussia
1785	The first U.S. minister to the Court of St James
1787	Publishes *A Defence of the Constitutions of Government of the United States*
1788	John and Abigail return home to Massachusetts (Quincy)
May 16, 1789 – March 4, 1797	Vice-president of the United States. He would cast 29 tie-breaking votes in the Senate.
1796	Denounces Thomas Paine's anti-Christian views in *The Age of Reason*
March 4, 1797 – March 4, 1801	President of the United States
1797/98	• *XYZ Affair*, in which the French demanded bribes from American diplomats to secure peace. The Americans refused, and this led to the undeclared or *Quasi-War* between the U.S. And France. • Estrangement from Thomas Jefferson, who did not share Adams' Federalist views, and who had supported the French Revolution
1798	• Signs Alien and Sedition Acts into law • *Direct Tax of 1798* passed to help fund a build-up of the U.S. Army and navy
1800	• First President to occupy the White House (November 1, 1800) • Nominates John Marshall as Chief Justice of the United States • Convention of 1800 creates peace between the U.S. And France • Son Charles dies of alcoholism
1812	Reconciliation with Thomas Jefferson
October 28, 1818	Abigail Adams dies of typhoid
1825/29	President John Quincy Adams
July 4, 1826	Adams dies at Peacefield in Quincy (Braintree) Massachusetts. Thomas Jefferson died on the same day. Adams is buried in United First Parish Church in Quincy.

Date	Events
1850/56	*The Works of John Adams, Esq., Second President of the United States*, edited by Charles Francis Adams is published
2001	*John Adams* is published by David McCullough
March 2008	*John Adams* miniseries debuts on HBO, with Paul Giamatti portraying John Adams

"Portrait of John Adams, painted by Mather Brown", 1788[1]

Other than perhaps Washington himself, is there any founder with a more impressive resume than John Adams? His list of accomplishments are prodigious, and he as much as anyone can take credit for the independence of the United States of America.

---

[1] Public domain.

A lawyer by trade, he successfully defended the British soldiers arrested for the Boston Massacre. Six were found not guilty, and two convicted of manslaughter.

As a member of both the first and second Continental Congresses, he was part of the committee that drew up the Declaration of Independence (ratified July 4, 1776). It is John Adams that, in June 1775, nominated George Washington of Virginia to be Commander in Chief.

He would serve as a diplomat in France during the Revolutionary War, and then achieve recognition of the United States as an independent government from the Dutch Republic. During his time in the Netherlands, he also procured a loan of 5,000,000 guilders. He would go on to become the first United States Ambassador to the Court of St. James in England at the War's end.

In 1789, he became the first Vice-President of the United States. He would cast 29 tie-breaking votes in the Senate.

In 1797, he would become the second President of the United States, and the first one to occupy the White House. He would serve only one term, before being defeated for the presidency by his sometimes friend Thomas Jefferson.

He was a prodigious and influential writer. His many writings during the period leading up to the Revolutionary War helped establish the intellectual basis for the separation from England. Among his most influential works:

- In *Novanglus; or, A History of the Dispute with America, From Its Origin, in 1754, to the Present Time*, Adams disputed the Parliament's authority over the colonies (1775)

- *Thoughts on Government*, written by Adams and published by Richard Henry Lee, became a reference for states developing state constitutions. The document supports a bicameral legislature, republicanism and separation of powers. (April 1776)
- Adams helped draft (with Samuel Adams and James Bowdoin) the Massachusetts Constitution (1779)
- *A Defense of the Constitutions of Government of the United States* (1787)

His time as President of the United States was a mixed bag. He successfully avoided a war with France, but was constantly fighting with fellow Federalists such as Alexander Hamilton. He also constantly fought with his Vice-President Thomas Jefferson, who belonged tho the Democratic-Republican Party. He built up the army and navy of the United States, and signed the Alien and Sedition Acts into law. Perhaps his most long-lasting accomplishment was nominating John Marshall as Chief Justice of the United States.

Over the years, John Adams often been relegated to a sort of second-tier of the Founding fathers. However, he clearly belongs in the first tier, and the 2001 biography *John Adams* by David McCullough, and the March 2008 HBO miniseries based on the McCullough book have helped re-cement his stature in the eyes of the public.

Between his published books and tracts, and his correspondence with his wife, and with Thomas Jefferson, we have many examples of his writings. In his *Novanglus, and Massachusettensis*, he disputed the Parliament's authority over the colonies:

> Now let me ask you, if the parliament of Great Britain, had all the natural foundations of authority, wisdom, goodness, justice, power, in as great perfection as they ever existed in any body of

men since Adam's fall; and if the English nation was the most virtuous, pure and free, that ever was; would not such an unlimited subjection of three millions of people to that parliament, at three thousand miles distance be real slavery? There are but two sorts of men in the world, freemen and slaves. The very definition of a freeman, is one who is bound by no law to which he has not consented. Americans would have no way of giving or withholding their consent to the acts of this parliament, therefore they would not be freemen. But, when luxury, effeminacy and venality are arrived at such a shocking pitch in England, when both electors and elected, are become one mass of corruption, when the nation is oppressed to death with debts and taxes, owing to their own extravagance, and want of wisdom, what would be your condition under such an absolute subjection to parliament? You would not only be slaves. But the most abject sort of slaves to the worst sort of masters! at least this is my opinion...

...They know that all America is united in sentiment, and in the plan of opposition to the claims of administration and parliament. The junto in Boston, with their little flocks of adherents in the country, are not worth taking into the account; and the army and navy, though these are divided among themselves, are no part of America; in order to judge of this union, they begin at the commencement of the dispute, and run through the whole course of it. At the time of the Stamp Act, every Colony expressed its sentiments by resolves of their assemblies, and every one agreed that parliament had no right to tax the Colonies. The house of representatives of the Massachusetts Bay, then consisted of many persons, who have since figured as friends to government; yet every member of that house concurred most cheerfully in the resolves then passed. The congress which met that year at New York, expressed the same opinion in their resolves, after the paint, paper and tea act was passed. The several assemblies expressed the same sentiments, and when your Colony wrote the famous circular letter, notwithstanding all the mandates and threats, and cajoling of the minister and the several governors, and all the crown officers through the continent, the assemblies with one voice echoed their entire approbation of that letter, and their applause to your Colony for sending it. In the year 1768, when a non importation was suggested and planned by a few gentlemen at a private club, in one of our large towns, as soon as it was proposed to the public, did it not spread through the whole continent?[2] (*Novanglus, and Massachusettensis*, John Adams, 1775)

In his *Thoughts on Government*, Adams provided a model for states developing state constitutions. In the excerpt below, he sings the praises of a Republican form of government.

A man must be indifferent to the sneers of modern Englishmen, to mention in their company the names of Sidney, Harrington, Locke, Milton, Nedham, Neville, Burnet, and Hoadly. No small fortitude is necessary to confess that one has read them. The wretched condition of this country, however, for ten or fifteen years past, has frequently reminded me of their principles and reasonings. They will convince any candid mind, that there is no good government but what is republican. That the only valuable part of the British constitution is so; because the very definition of a republic is "an empire of laws, and not of men." That, as a republic is the best of governments, so that particular arrangement of the powers of society, or, in other words, that form of government which is best contrived to secure an impartial and exact execution of the laws, is the best of republics...

...As good government is an empire of laws, how shall your laws be made? In a large society, inhabiting an extensive country, it is impossible that the whole should assemble to make laws. The first necessary step, then, is to depute power from the many to a few of the most wise and good. But by what rules shall you choose your representatives? Agree upon the number and qualifications of persons who shall have the benefit of choosing, or annex this privilege to the inhabitants of a certain extent of ground.

The principal difficulty lies, and the greatest care should be employed, in constituting this representative assembly. It should be in miniature an exact portrait of the people at large. It should think, feel, reason, and act like them. That it may be the interest of this assembly to do strict justice at all times, it should be an equal representation, or, in other words, equal interests among the people should have equal interests in it...[3] (*Thoughts on Government,* John Adams, April 1776)

[2]   http://www.gutenberg.org/files/45205/45205-h/45205-h.htm
[3]   http://www.constitution.org/jadams/thoughts.htm

Our final excerpt is from his 1797 Inaugural Address, in which he sings the praises of the United States Constitution.

Employed in the service of my country abroad during the whole course of these transactions, I first saw the Constitution of the United States in a foreign country. Irritated by no literary altercation, animated by no public debate, heated by no party animosity, I read it with great satisfaction, as the result of good heads prompted by good hearts, as an experiment better adapted to the genius, character, situation, and relations of this nation and country than any which had ever been proposed or suggested. In its general principles and great outlines it was conformable to such a system of government as I had ever most esteemed, and in some States, my own native State in particular, had contributed to establish. Claiming a right of suffrage, in common with my fellow-citizens, in the adoption or rejection of a constitution which was to rule me and my posterity, as well as them and theirs, I did not hesitate to express my approbation of it on all occasions, in public and in private. It was not then, nor has been since, any objection to it in my mind that the Executive and Senate were not more permanent. Nor have I ever entertained a thought of promoting any alteration in it but such as the people themselves, in the course of their experience, should see and feel to be necessary or expedient, and by their representatives in Congress and the State legislatures, according to the Constitution itself, adopt and ordain.

Returning to the bosom of my country after a painful separation from it for ten years, I had the honor to be elected to a station under the new order of things, and I have repeatedly laid myself under the most serious obligations to support the Constitution. The operation of it has equaled the most sanguine expectations of its friends, and from an habitual attention to it, satisfaction in its administration, and delight in its effects upon the peace, order, prosperity, and happiness of the nation I have acquired an habitual attachment to it and veneration for it.

What other form of government, indeed, can so well deserve our esteem and love?[4] (John Adams Inaugural Address, March 4, 1797)

---

[4]   http://www.bartleby.com/124/pres15.html

Samuel Adams

Date	Events
September 27, 1722	Born in Boston, Massachusetts
1740	Graduates from Harvard
1743	Master's Degree from Harvard
1747	Elected to a position of clerk in a Boston market
January 1748	Begins publishing the *Independent Advertiser*, a weekly newspaper that published many political tracts by Adams
October 1749	Marries Elizabeth Checkley. They would have 6 children (2 survived to adulthood).
1756	Elected tax collector
July 1757	Elizabeth Checkley Adams dies during childbirth
1764	• Marries Elizabeth Wells. They would have no children. • British pass the Sugar Act. Adams begins arguing against taxation without representation
May 24, 1764	Boston Town Meeting adopts Adams' views on no taxation without representation
1765	Stamp Act passed (a tax on printed materials). Adams would argue that humanity had certain *natural rights* that could not be abridged by a government.
1766/74	Clerk of the Massachusetts House of Representatives
May 16, 1766	The Stamp Act is repealed, after most tax collectors are pressured into resigning
1767	Townshend Acts passed
February 1768	Publishes the *Massachusetts Circular Letter*, which is passed by the Massachusetts House of Representatives. They are in opposition to the British Townshend Acts.
October 1768	British occupy Boston
March 5, 1770	Boston Massacre
April 1770	Parliament rescinds the Townshend duties, except the one on tea

Date	Events
April 1772	Adams reelected to the Massachusetts House
November 1772	Adams leads the formation of the *committee of correspondence* system throughout the 13 colonies
May 1773	Adams reelected to the Massachusetts House
June 1773	• Adams presents letters to the House written by Governor Thomas Hutchinson, seemingly calling for an "abridgment" of liberties in Massachusetts • Tea Act passed, allowing the East India Company to sell tea directly to the colonies, rather than going through Colonial middlemen
November 29, 1773	Adams calls for a mass meeting at the Old South Meeting House on the Tea Act
December 16, 1773	Boston Tea Party
1774	Intolerable Acts (Coercive Acts) passed against Massachusetts
March 31, 1774	Boston Port Act (part of the Coercive Acts) passed. It was, essentially, a blockade of the Boston port.
September 5, 1774	Member of the First Continental Congress
November 1774	Serves in the Massachusetts Provincial Congress
April 18, 1775	Adams escapes arrest from General Gage, who sends troops to Lexington and Concord
May 10, 1775	Member of the Second Continental Congress
July 4, 1776	Signs Declaration of Independence
1777	Member of the *Board of War*, which oversees the Continental Army on behalf of Congress
1778	Signs the Articles of Confederation (formerly ratified in 1781)
1779	Helps draft (with John Adams and James Bowdoin) the Massachusetts Constitution
1780	Charter member of the American Academy of Arts and Sciences
1781	Retires from the Continental Congress
1782/85	President of the Massachusetts Senate
1786	Supports military action against Shays's Rebellion
January 1788	Supports the new United States Constitution at the Massachusetts ratifying convention, but has

Date	Events
	concerns over too much federal control
1787/88	President of the Massachusetts Senate
December 1788	Loses U.S. House of representatives election to Fisher Ames
1789/94	Lieutenant Governor of Massachusetts
December 15, 1791	Bill of Rights ratified by the states; Adams was a strong supporter
1794	Supports military action against the Whiskey Rebellion
1794/797	Governor of Massachusetts
1796	Receives 15 electoral votes in Virginia for president
1865	His great-grandson William Wells writes a three-volume biography of Samuel Adams entitled *The Life and Public Services of Samuel Adams*
October 2, 1803	Dies in Cambridge, Massachusetts of *Essential tremor;* he is buried at the Granary Burying Ground in Boston
1985	Samuel Adams Boston Lager is released

The time line of Samuel Adams (second cousin to John Adams) is, essentially, the time line of the American Revolution. Perhaps no other figure played as great a role in bringing about the separation from Britain than Adams. (Picture: Portrait of Samuel Adams by John Singleton Copley[5])

He was a publisher, a politician, a political organizer and a rabble-rouser. He was the guiding force for setting up the original *committee of correspondence* system throughout the 13 colonies. He was a member of both the First and Second

[5] Public domain.   Museum of Fine Arts, Boston .

Continental Congresses. He served (variously) as a member of the Massachusetts House, a member of the Board of War that oversaw the Continental Army for Congress, a member of the Massachusetts Provincial Congress, President of the Massachusetts Senate, Lieutenant Governor of Massachusetts, and, finally, as Governor of Massachusetts.

He is closely associated with both the Boston Massacre (one viewpoint is that he helped instigate it), and the Boston Tea Party (which he also helped instigate). He was closely associated with the Sons of Liberty. He fought against every new British tax of the 1760s and 1770s.

"The bloody massacre perpetrated in King Street Boston on March 5th 1770 by a party of the 29th Regt." From an engraving by Paul Revere.[6]

---

[6]   Library of Congress http://www.loc.gov/pictures/item/2008661777/

He was a strong supporter of the Declaration of Independence the Articles of Confederation, and the Bill of Rights. He signed the Constitution of the United States perhaps more reluctantly, because he thought it took power away from the states and gave it to the Federal government.

Several excerpts from his letters allow us some view into his thinking. The following letter of April 10, 1773, discusses the early days of the establishment of the committees of correspondence (a precursor to the First Continental Congress). Adams was instrumental in establishing the Committees.

The Friends of Liberty in this Town have lately made a successful Attempt to obtain the explicit political Sentiments of a great Number of the Towns in this Province; and the Number is daily increasing. The very Attempt was alarming to the Adversaries; and the happy Effects of it are mortifying to them. I would propose it for your Consideration, Whether the Establishment of Committees of Correspondence among the several Towns in every Colony, would not tend to promote that General Union, upon which the Security of the whole depends.

The Reception of the truly patriotick Resolves of the House of Burgesses of Virginia gladdens the Hearts of all who are Friends to Liberty. Our Committee of Correspondence had a special Meeting upon this Occasion, and determined immediately to circulate printed Copies in every Town in this Province, in order to make them as extensively useful as possible. I am desired by them to assure you of their Veneration for your most ancient Colony, and their unfeigned Esteem for the Gentlemen of your Committee. This indeed is a small Return; I hope you will have the hearty Concurrence of every Assembly on the Continent. It is a Measure that I think must be attended with great and good Consequences.[7]

In June 1773, Adams presented letters to the House written by Governor Thomas Hutchinson, seemingly calling for an

---

[7] *The Writings of Samuel Adams: 1773-1777, Volume III*, by Samuel Adams (G. P. Putnam's Sons, 1907)

"abridgment" of liberties in Massachusetts. Here he discusses those letters in a letter to Arthur Lee.

TO ARTHUR LEE.

Boston, June 14th, [1773.]

Dear Sir, I now enclose letters written by Thomas Hutchinson and Oliver and others of less importance, the originals of which have been laid before the house of representatives. The house have already resolved, by a majority of 101 out of 106 members, that the design and tendency of them is to subvert the constitution and introduce arbitrary power into the province. They are now in the hands of a committee to consider them farther, and report what is still proper to be done.

I think there is now a full discovery of a combination of persons who have been the principal movers, in all the disturbance, misery, and bloodshed, which has befallen this unhappy country. The friends of our great men are much chagrined.

I am much engaged at present, and will write you more fully by the next opportunity. In the mean time believe me to be with great esteem your unfeigned friend...[8]

In this letter from January 1774, Adams discusses his views on the Tea Act and the destruction of tea in Boston Harbor, and apportions blame for the act..

TO ARTHUR LEE.

Jan 25 1774

The sending the East India Companies Tea into America appears evidently to have been with Design of the British Administration, and to complete the favorite plan of establishing a Revenue in America. The People of Boston and the other adjacent Towns endeavored to have the Tea sent back to the place from whence it came & then to prevent the Design from taking Effect. Had this

---

[8] *The Writings of Samuel Adams: 1773-1777, Volume III*, by Samuel Adams (G. P. Putnam's Sons, 1907)

been done in Boston, as it was done in New York & Philadelphia, the Design of the Ministry would have been as effectually prevented here as in those Colonies and the property would have been saved. Governor Hutchinson & the other Crown officers having the Command of the Castle by which the Ships must have passed, & other powers in their Hands, made use of these Powers to defeat the Intentions of the people & succeeded; in short the Governor who for Art & Cunning as well as an inveterate hatred of the people was inferior to no one of the Cabal; both encouraged & provoked the people to destroy the Tea. By refusing to grant a Passport he held up to them the alternative of destroying the property of the East India Company or suffering that to be the sure means of unhinging the Security of property in general in America, and by delaying to call on the naval power to protect the Tea, he led them to determine their Choice of Difficulties. In this View of the Matter the Question is easily decided who ought in Justice to pay for the Tea if it ought to be paid for at all.

The Destruction of the Tea is the pretense for the unprecedented Severity shown to the Town of Boston but **the real Cause is the opposition to Tyranny for which the people of that Town have always made themselves remarkable & for which I think this Country is much obliged to them. They are suffering the Vengeance of Administration in the Common Cause of America.** (emphasis added) [9]

Adams was a great supporter of the Declaration of Independence. In the two extracts below, he urges the passage of such a Declaration before the fact (first excerpt), and expresses satisfaction after the Declaration is passed (second excerpt).

TO JOSEPH HAWLEY.

Philadelphia April 15 1776

...I am perfectly satisfied with the Reasons you offer to show the Necessity of a public & explicit Declaration of Independency. I cannot conceive what good Reason can be assigned against it. Will

---

[9] *The Writings of Samuel Adams: 1773-1777, Volume III*, by Samuel Adams (G. P. Putnam's Sons, 1907)

it widen the Breach? This would be a strange Question after we have raised Armies and fought Battles with the British Troops, set up an American Navy, permitted the Inhabitants of these Colonies to fit out armed Vessels to cruize on all Ships &c belonging to any of the Inhabitants of Great Britain declaring them the Enemies of the united Colonies, and torn into Shivers their Acts of Trade, by allowing Commerce subject to Regulations to be made by our selves with the People of all Countries but such as are Subjects of the British King. It cannot surely after all this be imagined that we consider our selves or mean to be considered by others in any State but that of Independence.[10]

TO RICHARD HENRY LEE.
Philadelphia July 15 1776

Our Declaration of Independency has given Vigor to the Spirits of the People. Had this decisive Measure been taken Nine Months ago, it is my opinion that Canada would at this time have been in our hands. But what does it avail to find fault with what is past. Let us do better for the future.[11]

---

[10] *The Writings of Samuel Adams: 1773-1777, Volume III*, by Samuel Adams (G. P. Putnam's Sons, 1907)
[11] *The Writings of Samuel Adams: 1773-1777, Volume III*, by Samuel Adams (G. P. Putnam's Sons, 1907)

Ethan Allen

Date	Events
January 21, 1738	Born in Litchfield, Connecticut
1757	Joins the militia during the French and Indian War
July 1762	Marries Mary Brownson in Roxbury, Connecticut (d. 1783 of tuberculosis)
1762	Part owner of an iron furnace in Salisbury, Connecticut (sold out in October 1765)
1766	Invests in a lead mine in Northampton, Massachusetts
July 1770	Represents interests of landowners west of the Connecticut River (*The New Hampshire Grants*) before the New York Supreme Court and loses; shortly afterwards, Allen is elected colonel of the Green Mountain Boys militia
October 1771	Allen and the Green Mountain Boys burn cabins of immigrants from New York near Rupert, Vermont
1772	Allen and various relatives form the Onion River Company, a real estate speculation company. One part of the land they purchased and later sold became Burlington.
March 1774	Rewards of up to 100 pounds for the capture of the Green Mountain Boys
Summer 1774	Allen writes *A Brief Narrative of the Proceedings of the Government of New York Relative to Their Obtaining the Jurisdiction of that Large District of Land to the Westward of the Connecticut River*
May 9, 1775	Benedict Arnold joins Ethan Allen as head of the Fort Ticonderoga mission
May 10, 1775	Ethan Allen and his Green Mountain Boys (about 83 men) seize Fort Ticonderoga
May 12, 1775	Green Mountain Boys under Captain Seth Warner capture Fort Crown Point at Lake Champlain, New York
May 14, 1775	Green Mountain Boys under Ethan Allen capture the sloop *HMS Royal George*; an ensuing raid on Fort St. John on the Richelieu River is unsuccessful

Date	Events
June 22, 1775	Allen and Seth Warner appear before the Congress in Philadelphia, requesting that the Green Mountain Boys be integrated into the Continental Army; the request is approved. Shortly after, the newly installed regiment elected Seth Warner as their commander, dissing Allen.
September 4, 1775	On the way to assault Montreal, the Continental Army begins a siege of Fort St. John; Allen is sent ahead to enlist support from the people of Quebec. He eventually raises a force of 200 Quebec-ian volunteers.
September 25, 1775	Captured by the British in an assault on Montreal at the Battle of Longue-Pointe
January 15, 1777	Vermont declares independence
1778	After being imprisoned on various ships and in Cornwall, England, Allen is released in a prisoner exchange. He reports to Washington at Valley Forge.
May 14, 1778	Promoted to Brevet Colonel in the Continental Army, but is not given a command
May 25, 1778	Returns to Vermont
September 1778	Appears before the Continental Congress, speaking on behalf of Vermont statehood
1779	Writes *A Narrative of Colonel Ethan Allen's Captivity … Containing His Voyages and Travels, With the most remarkable Occurrences respecting him and many other Continental Prisoners of Observations. Written by Himself and now published for the Information of the Curious in all Nations*
1785	Releases *Reason: the Only Oracle of Man*, an anti-Christian screed; only 200 copies were sold
February 16, 1784	Marries "Fanny" Montresor Brush Buchanan; they would have three children
1787	Moves to Burlington, Vermont from Bennington, Vermont
February 12, 1789	Dies in Burlington, Vermont of a stroke; he was buried at the Green Mount Cemetery in Burlington.
March 4, 1791	Vermont becomes a state
October 3,	*USS Ethan Allen* commissioned

Date	Events
1861	
August 16, 1942	Liberty Ship USS Ethan Allen launched (scrapped 1960)
1955	3 cent stamp depicting Ethan Allen and Fort Ticonderoga is released by the U.S. Post Office
November 22, 1960	Ballistic missile submarine USS Ethan Allen launched (decommissioned 31 March 1983; scrapped 1999)
December 1996	Amtrak Ethan Allen Express begins service between New York City and Rutland, Vermont (via Albany, New York)
1988	Art Deco-style Ethan Allen School in Philadelphia added to the National Register of Historic Places

"A Map of Ticonderoga with the old and new lines and batteries, taken from an actual survey & other authentick informations, 1777"[12]

Ethan Allen was a farmer, soldier, insurgent, author, politician and supporter of the weak. He was also a real estate speculator, a foe of Christianity, and a guerrilla that burned

---

[12] Library of Congress http://hdl.loc.gov/loc.gmd/g3804t.ar117500

down the cabins of settlers in what is modern day Vermont. But today he is remembered mostly for what happened on May 10, 1775, when Allen and his Green Mountain Boys (83 men) seized massive Fort Ticonderoga. When asked by the commander of the fort under what authority he was seizing the fort, Allen (who had a certain grandiosity of speech) replied with the immortal words, "In the name of the great Jehovah, and the Continental Congress."

In 1779, Allen wrote down his account of the attack on Fort Ticonderoga:

> ...directions were privately sent to me from the then colony, (now state) of Connecticut, to raise the Green Mountain Boys, and, if possible, to surprise and take the fortress of Ticonderoga. This enterprise I cheerfully undertook; and, after first guarding all the several passes that led thither, to cut off all intelligence between the garrison and the country, made a forced march from Bennington, and arrived at the lake opposite to Ticonderoga, on the evening of the ninth day of May, 1775, with two hundred and thirty valiant Green Mountain Boys; and it was with the utmost difficulty that I procured boats to cross the lake. However, I landed eighty-three men near the garrison, and sent the boats back for the rear guard, commanded by Col. Seth Warner, but the day began to dawn, and I found myself under a necessity to attack the fort, before the rear could cross the lake; and, as it was viewed hazardous, I harangued the officers and soldiers in the manner following:
>
> "Friends and fellow soldiers, You have, for a number of years past been a scourge and terror to arbitrary power. Your valor has been famed abroad, and acknowledged, as appears by the advice and orders to me, from the General Assembly of Connecticut, to surprise and take the garrison now before us. I now propose to advance before you, and in person, conduct you through the wicket-gate; for we must this morning either quit our pretensions to valor, or possess ourselves of this fortress in a few minutes; and, inasmuch as it is a desperate attempt, which none but the bravest of men dare undertake, I do not urge it on any contrary to his will. You that will undertake voluntarily, poise your firelocks."

The men being, at this time, drawn up in three ranks, each poised his firelock. I ordered them to face to the right, and at the head of the centre-file, marched them immediately to the wicket-gate aforesaid, where I found a sentry posted, who instantly snapped his fusee [light musket] at me; I ran immediately towards him, and he retreated through the covered way into the parade within the garrison, gave a halloo, and ran under a bombproof. My party, who followed me into the fort, I formed on the parade in such a manner as to face the two barracks which faced each other.

The garrison being asleep, except the sentries, we gave three huzzas which greatly surprised them. One of the sentries made a pass at one of my officers with a charged bayonet, and slightly wounded him: My first thought was to kill him with my sword; but in an instant, I altered the design and fury of the blow to a slight cut on the side of the head; upon which he dropped his gun, and asked quarter, which I readily granted him, and demanded of him the place where the commanding officer kept; he showed me a pair of stairs in the front of a barrack, on the west part of the garrison, which led up a second story in said barrack, to which I immediately repaired, and ordered the commander, Capt. De La Place, to come forth instantly, or I would sacrifice the whole garrison; at which the Capt. came immediately to the door with his breeches in his hand; when I ordered him to deliver me the fort instantly; he asked me by what authority I demanded it; I answered him **"In the name of the great Jehovah, and the Continental Congress."** The authority of the Congress being very little known at that time, he began to speak again; but I interrupted him, and with my drawn sword over his head, again demanded an immediate surrender of the garrison; with which he then complied, and ordered his men to be forthwith paraded without arms, as he had given up the garrison. In the mean time some of my officers had given orders, and in consequence thereof, sundry of the barrack doors were beat down, and about one third of the garrison imprisoned, which consisted of the said commander, a Lieut. Feltham, a conducter of artillery, a gunner, two sergeants, and forty-four rank and file; about one hundred pieces of cannon, one thirteen inch mortar, and a number of swivels. This surprise was carried into execution in the grey of the morning of the tenth day of May, 1775. The sun seemed to rise that morning with a superior lustre; and Ticonderoga and its dependencies smiled on its conquerors, who tossed about the flowing bowl, and wished success to Congress, and the liberty and freedom of America. Happy it was for me, at that time, that the then future pages of the book of fate, which afterwards unfolded a miserable scene of two years and eight months imprisonment, were hid from my view.[13] (Ethan Allen, 1779; emphasis added)

On September 25, 1775, Allen led an ill-fated assault on Montreal at the Battle of Longue-Pointe. Allen was captured, and spent the next 2+ years being imprisoned on various ships and in Cornwall, England. In 1778, he was released in a prisoner exchange. Below is his account of his capture at Longue-Pointe.

The fire continued for some time on both sides; and I was confident that such a remote method of attack could not carry the ground, provided it should be continued till night; but near half the body of the enemy began to flank round to my right; upon which I ordered a volunteer, by the name of John Dugan, who had lived many years in Canada, and understood the French language, to detach about fifty of the Canadians, and post himself at an advantageous ditch, which was on my right, to prevent my being surrounded: He advanced with the detachment, but instead of occupying the post, made his escape, as did likewise Mr. Young upon the left, with their detachments. I soon perceived that the enemy was in the possession of the ground, which Dugan should have occupied. At this time I had but about forty-five men with me; some of whom were wounded; the enemy kept closing round me, nor was it in my power to prevent it; by which means, my situation, which was advantageous in the first part of the attack, ceased to be so in the last; and being almost entirely surrounded with such vast unequal numbers, I ordered a retreat, but found that those of the enemy, who were of the country, and their Indians, could run as fast as my men, though the regulars could not. Thus I retreated near a mile, and some of the enemy, with the savages, kept flanking me, and others crowded hard in the rear. In fine [in the end], I expected, in a very short time to try the world of spirits; for I was apprehensive that no quarter would be given me, and therefore had determined to sell my life as dear as I could. One of the enemy's officers, boldly pressing in the rear,

[13] *Ethan Allen's Narrative of the Capture of Ticonderoga: And of His Captivity and Treatment by the British,* by Ethan Allen (C. Goodrich & S. B. Nichols, 1849)

discharged his fusee at me; the ball whistled near me, as did many others that day. I returned the salute, and missed him, as running had put us both out of breath: for I conclude we were not frightened: I then saluted him with my tongue in a harsh manner, and told him that, inasmuch as his numbers were far superior to mine, I would surrender provided I could be treated with honor, and be assured of good quarters for myself and the men who were with me; and he answered I should; another officer, coming up directly after, confirmed the treaty; upon which I agreed to surrender with my party, which then consisted of thirty-one effective men, and seven wounded. I ordered them to ground their arms, which they did.

The officer I capitulated with, then directed me and my party to advance towards him, which was done; I handed him my sword...[14] (Ethan Allen, 1779)

His capture of Fort Ticonderoga with such a small force early in the war helped boost Colonial morale, at least for a while.

---

[14] *Ethan Allen's Narrative of the Capture of Ticonderoga: And of His Captivity and Treatment by the British,* by Ethan Allen (C. Goodrich & S. B. Nichols, 1849)

Ethan Allen before Captain Prescott, 1775[15]

---

[15] Published November 1902 in *Century Magazine*. Public domain.

Benjamin Franklin

While a case could be made that George Washington had the greatest effect on the outcome of the American Revolution, a case can also be made that the American who had the most impact on American (colonial and United States) in the 18th century overall was Benjamin Franklin. He was an inventor and scientist, author, publisher, politician, diplomat, a civic giant and a revolutionary. Probably no one since Leonardo DaVinci had such varied and impact-ful skills.

"Benjamin Franklin - born in Boston, Jany. 17th 1706 -- died in Philadelphia, April 17th 1790"[16]

[16] Library of Congress http://www.loc.gov/pictures/item/2006676692/

Date	Events
January 17, 1706	Born in Boston
1722	Briefly acts as publisher of the *The New-England Courant* while his brother is in jail for dissing the governor; publishes letters under the pseudonym *Mrs. Silence Dogood*
1723	Runs away to Philadelphia
1729	• Editor of the *Pennsylvania Gazette* • Published *A Modest Enquiry into the Nature and Necessity of a Paper Currency in 1729*
1730	Appointed public printer
September 1, 1730	Common law marriage with Deborah Read (whose husband had absconded with her dowry to Barbados). They would have two children (and raise Franklin's illegitimate son William).
1731	Founds the first Philadelphia Library
1732/58	Publishes *Poor Richard's Almanac*, under the pseudonym Richard Saunders
1732	Founds the first German language newspaper in America – *Die Philadelphische Zeitung*
1734	Grand Master of the Philadelphia Freemasons
1736	Founds the first Philadelphia Fire Company (*Union Fire Company*)
1737	Postmaster of Philadelphia
1738	Member of the Provincial Assembly
1741	Establishes *The General Magazine and Historical Chronicle for all the British Plantations in America*, the first monthly magazine in America
1742	• Invents the Franklin Open Stove • Becomes official printer for the Moravians of Bethlehem, Pennsylvania
1743	Founds the American Philosophical Society
June 25, 1745	Writes letter *Advice to a Friend on Choosing a Mistress*
October 1748	Philadelphia city councilman
1749	• Founds The Academy and College of Philadelphia (later, the University of Pennsylvania) • Invents the lightning rod

Date	Events
1750	Publishes a proposal on how to prove lightning is electricity - by flying a kite in a storm
1751	• Founds the Pennsylvania Hospital (where I was born) • Appointed a Justice of the Peace for Philadelphia
June 15, 1752	Flies a kite in a storm. Franklin's experiments would lead to the identification of positive and negative charge and electrical grounding
1753	• Appointed Deputy Postmaster for the Colonies • Receives Royal Society's Copley Medal for his work with electricity • Awarded honorary degree by Harvard University • Awarded honorary degree by Yale University
1754	Delegate to the Congress at Albany, New York (a meeting of delegates from Connecticut, Maryland, Massachusetts, New Hampshire, New York, Pennsylvania, and Rhode Island)
1755	Publishes *Observations on the Increase of Mankind*, which helped create the science of demography
1756	• Establishes the Pennsylvania Militia, and elected Colonel • Elected as a Fellow of the Royal Society
1757/70	Agent to Great Britain for Pennsylvania, Georgia, New Jersey and Massachusetts
1758	• Publishes *Father Abraham's Sermon*, also known as *The Way to Wealth* • Experiments with refrigeration by using evaporation cooling
February 1759	Awarded an Honorary Doctor of Laws degree by the University of St Andrews
1762	Awarded honorary doctorate by Oxford University
1763	• William Franklin appointed Royal Governor of New Jersey • Benjamin Franklin raises the local militia to defend Philadelphia from angry settlers involved in Pontiac's Rebellion
1764	Speaker of the Pennsylvania Assembly
1766	Speaks to the British Parliament against new taxes

Date	Events
	for the colonies as a result of the French and Indian War
1767	Co-founder of the *Pennsylvania Chronicle and Universal Advertiser*
1768	Produces *A Scheme for a New Alphabet and a Reformed Mode of Spelling* – a phonetic alphabet
1769	President of the American Philosophical Society
1770	• Publishes Gulf Stream chart in Britain. A copy of this was discovered in the *Bibliothèque Nationale* in Paris in 1980. • Franklin's slaves had been freed
1771	Begins writing his autobiography
1772	Defines a decision-making tool called the "Pro and Con" list
1773	• Publishes *Rules by Which a Great Empire May Be Reduced to a Small One* • Publishes *An Edict by the King of Prussia*
June 1773	Obtains private letters of Thomas Hutchinson, and sends them to Boston, where they are gleefully published by Samuel Adams
1774	Deborah Read Franklin dies of a stroke
1775	• Delegate to the Continental Congress • Chairman of the Committee of Safety • Proposed *Articles of Confederation and Perpetual Union* • Postmaster General of the Colonies (July 26, 1775)
1776	• Signs the Declaration of Independence, after being part of the Committee of Five that prepared it • President of the Constitutional Convention of Pennsylvania • Commissioner to the Court of France • Begins wearing bifocals, which he probably invented
1778	• Negotiated treaties of Amity and Commerce and of Alliance with France • Minister Plenipotentiary to France
February 4,	French give ship *Duc de Duras* (1765) to John Paul

Date	Events
1779	Jones, who renames it *USS Bonhomme Richard* (*Poor Richard*)
1779/81	Grand Master of the *Les Neuf Sœurs* Freemasons
1783	• Signed Treaty of Amity and Commerce with Sweden • Signed Treaty of Peace with Great Britain
1785	• Signed Treaty of Amity and Commerce with Prussia
1785/88	Governor (President) of Pennsylvania
1786	His *Maritime Observations* is published by the Philosophical Society
December 1786	His *The Morals of Chess* is published in *Columbian* magazine
1787	• Member of the Constitutional Convention • Franklin College (now Franklin & Marshall College) named in his honor
1788	Completes his autobiography
1789	Writes two anti-slavery tracts: • *An Address to the Public* • *A Plan for Improving the Condition of the Free Blacks*
1790	Writes anti-slavery tract *Sidi Mehemet Ibrahim on the Slave Trade*
April 17, 1790	Dies in Philadelphia of pleurisy (an inflammation of the lungs). He was buried in Christ Church Burial Ground in Philadelphia.
August 1815	74-gun ship of the line *USS Franklin* launched
1824	The Franklin Institute opens in Philadelphia
1847	Franklin appears on the first U.S. Postage stamp (5¢)
1861	1¢ Benjamin Franklin stamp issued
1895	• 1¢ Benjamin Franklin stamp issued • Franklin Field opens in Philadelphia, home of the University of Pennsylvania football team
1908/23	Washington-Franklin stamp issues
1917	*Benjamin Franklin Parkway* constructed in Philadelphia
July 1, 1926	Benjamin Franklin Bridge over the Delaware opens
1928	Franklin's image is placed on the $100 bill

Date	Events
October 14, 1943	USS Franklin (CV-13) aircraft carrier launched
April 29, 1944	USS Bon Homme Richard (CV-31) launched (Poor Richard)
1948/63	Franklin appears on the U.S. half dollar
1956	Royal Society of Arts creates a Benjamin Franklin Medal
December 5, 1964	Ballistic submarine USS Benjamin Franklin (SSBN-640) launched
October 25, 1972	Benjamin Franklin National Memorial, in the Franklin Institute
1999	Inducted into the U.S. Chess Hall of Fame
January 17, 2006	Benjamin Franklin House museum on Craven Street in London opens

As an **inventor/scientist**, his accomplishments were prodigious enough to have him made a a Fellow of the Royal Society. He also received honorary degrees from Harvard University (1753), Yale University (1753), University of St Andrews (1759) and Oxford University (1762). His honorary degree from St. Andrews was a doctorate, so from that point on, Franklin often referred to himself as "Dr. Franklin".

Among his accomplishments:

- Invents the Franklin Open Stove (1742)
- Invents the lightning rod (1749)
- Publishes a proposal on how to prove lightning is electricity - by flying a kite in a storm (1750). His ongoing experiments with electricity would lead to the identification of positive and negative charge and the concept of electrical grounding.
- Receives Royal Society's Copley Medal for his work with electricity (1753)
- Experiments with refrigeration by using evaporation cooling (1758)

- Publishes Gulf Stream chart in Britain (1770). A copy of this was discovered in the Bibliothèque Nationale in Paris in 1980.
- Defines a decision-making tool called the "Pro and Con" list (1772)
- Begins wearing bifocals, which he probably invented (1776)
- His *Maritime Observations* is published by the Philosophical Society (1786)

As an **author**, Franklin wrote many tracts, papers and a book. Some of his works were on homespun wisdom, some on scientific matters, some on economics, and some on politics. Among his works:

- *A Modest Enquiry into the Nature and Necessity of a Paper Currency* (1729)
- *Observations on the Increase of Mankind* (1755), which helped create the science of demography
- *Father Abraham's Sermon*, also known as *The Way to Wealth* (1758)
- *A Scheme for a New Alphabet and a Reformed Mode of Spelling* (1768) – about proposing a phonetic alphabet

- *Rules by Which a Great Empire May Be Reduced to a Small One* (1773)
- *An Edict by the King of Prussia (1773)*
- *The Morals of Chess* (1786)
- *Autobiography of Benjamin Franklin* (1788)
- *An Address to the Public* (1789) – an anti-slavery tract
- *A Plan for Improving the Condition of the Free Blacks* - an anti-slavery tract
- *Sidi Mehemet Ibrahim on the Slave Trade* (1790) - an anti-slavery tract

As a **publisher**, Franklin established several newspapers and magazines, and also acted as the printer/publisher for the Moravians in Bethlehem, Pennsylvania. Among his newspaper and magazine ventures:

- *Pennsylvania Gazette* (1729)
- *Poor Richard's Almanac*, written under the pseudonym Richard Saunders (1732/58)
- *Die Philadelphische Zeitung* (1732) – the first German language newspaper in America
- *The General Magazine and Historical Chronicle for all the British Plantations in America* - the first monthly magazine in America (1741)
- *Pennsylvania Chronicle and Universal Advertiser* (1767)

As a **politician**, Franklin served as Governor (President) of Pennsylvania, as well as a delegate to various Continental political bodies. Among the positions he served:

- Member of the Provincial Assembly (1738)
- Philadelphia city councilman (October 1748)
- Delegate to the Congress at Albany, New York (1754) (a meeting of delegates from Connecticut, Maryland,

Massachusetts, New Hampshire, New York, Pennsylvania, and Rhode Island)
- Speaker of the Pennsylvania Assembly (1764)
- Delegate to the Continental Congress (1775)
  - Chairman of the Committee of Safety
  - Proposed "Articles of Confederation and Perpetual Union"
- President of the Constitutional Convention of Pennsylvania (1776)
- Governor (President) of Pennsylvania (1785/88)
- Member of the Constitutional Convention (1787)

It is in his role as a **diplomat** that Franklin had his biggest impact on the American revolution. He negotiated the alliance with France, and was a signer of the Peace Treaty with England. He also signed treaties with Sweden and Prussia.

- Agent to Great Britain for Pennsylvania, Georgia, New Jersey and Massachusetts (1757/70)
- Commissioner to the Court of France (1776)
- Negotiated treaties of Amity and Commerce and of Alliance with France (1778)
- Minister Plenipotentiary to France (1778)
- Signed Treaty of Amity and Commerce with Sweden (1783)
- Signed Treaty of Peace with Great Britain (1783)
- Signed Treaty of Amity and Commerce with Prussia (1785)

Franklin was the only person who signed the Declaration of Independence, the Alliance with France, the Peace Treaty with Great Britain, and the U.S. Constitution.

Franklin was a **civic giant** and his impact on Pennsylvania (and especially Philadelphia) was legendary. The first library. The first fire company. The first major college. The first hospital. Specifically:

- Founds the first Philadelphia Library (1731)
- Founds the first Philadelphia Fire Company (Union Fire Company) (1736)
- Founds the American Philosophical Society (1743)
- Founds The Academy and College of Philadelphia (later, the University of Pennsylvania) (1749)
- Founds the Pennsylvania Hospital (where I was born) (1751)

Among his other accomplishments, Franklin also served as a **civil servant** for both the British and for the Continental Congress.

- Postmaster of Philadelphia (1737)
- Appointed a Justice of the Peace for Philadelphia (1751)
- Appointed Deputy Postmaster for the Colonies (1753)
- Postmaster General of the Colonies (July 26, 1775)

And finally, Franklin was a **revolutionary** and **patriot**. As already noted, his greatest impact on the Revolution was the alliance with France, but he was also a member of the Committee of Five that created the Declaration of Independence, and he was also behind the publishing of private letters written by Massachusetts Governor Thomas Hutchinson. Franklin procured them in England, and sent them to Boston, where they were gleefully published by Samuel Adams.

Included below are several excerpts from the *Autobiography of Benjamin Franklin.* In the first, he describes how he created Poor Richard's Almanac:

IN 1732 I first publish'd my Almanack, under the name of Richard Saunders; it was continu'd by me about twenty-five years, commonly call'd Poor Richard's Almanac. I endeavour'd to make it both entertaining and useful, and it accordingly came to be in such demand, that I reap'd considerable profit from it, vending annually near ten thousand. And observing that it was generally read, scarce any neighborhood in the province being without it, I consider'd it as a proper vehicle for conveying instruction among the common people, who bought scarcely any other books; I therefore filled all the little spaces that occurr'd between the remarkable days in the calendar with proverbial sentences, chiefly such as inculcated industry and frugality, as the means of procuring wealth, and thereby securing virtue; it being more difficult for a man in want, to act always honestly, as, to use here one of those proverbs, it is hard for an empty sack to stand upright.[17]

Franklin discusses his experiments with electricity (first excerpt) in his *Autobiography*, and the impact (second excerpt) that those experiments had.

ELECTRICAL KITE

To Peter Collinson
[Philadelphia], Oct. 19, 1752.

Sir,

As frequent mention is made in public papers from Europe of the success of the Philadelphia experiment for drawing the electric fire from clouds by means of pointed rods of iron erected on high buildings, &c., it may be agreeable to the curious to be informed, that the same experiment has succeeded in Philadelphia, though made in a different and more easy manner, which is as follows:

Make a small cross of two light strips of cedar, the arms so long as to reach to the four corners of a large, thin silk handkerchief when extended; tie the corners of the handkerchief to the extremities of the cross, so you have the body of a kite; which being properly

[17] http://www.gutenberg.org/files/20203/20203-h/20203-h.htm#XVIII

accommodated with a tail, loop, and string, will rise in the air, like those made of paper; but this being of silk, is fitter to bear the wet and wind of a thunder-gust without tearing. To the top of the upright stick of the cross is to be fixed a very sharp-pointed wire, rising a foot or more above the wood. To the end of the twine, next the hand, is to be tied a silk ribbon, and where the silk and twine join, a key may be fastened. This kite is to be raised when a thunder-gust appears to be coming on, and the person who holds the string must stand within a door or window, or under some cover, so that the silk ribbon may not be wet; and care must be taken that the twine does not touch the frame of the door or window. As soon as any of the thunder clouds come over the kite, the pointed wire will draw the electric fire from them, and the kite, with all the twine will be electrified, and the loose filaments of the twine will stand out every way and be attracted by an approaching finger. And when the rain has wet the kite and twine, so that it can conduct the electric fire freely, you will find it stream out plentifully from the key on the approach of your knuckle. At this key the phial may be charged; and from electric fire thus obtained, spirits may be kindled, and all the electric experiments be performed, which are usually done by the help of a rubbed glass globe or tube, and thereby the sameness of the electric matter with that of lightning completely demonstrated.

B. Franklin.[18]

What gave my book the more sudden and general celebrity, was the success of one of its proposed experiments, made by Messrs. Dalibard and De Lor at Marly, for drawing lightning from the clouds. This engag'd the public attention everywhere. M. de Lor, who had an apparatus for experimental philosophy, and lectur'd in that branch of science, undertook to repeat what he called the Philadelphia Experiments; and, after they were performed before the king and court, all the curious of Paris flocked to see them. I will not swell this narrative with an account of that capital experiment, nor of the infinite pleasure I receiv'd in the success of a similar one I made soon after with a kite at Philadelphia, as both are to be found in the histories of electricity.[19]

---

[18] http://www.gutenberg.org/files/20203/20203-h/20203-h.htm#XVIII
[19] http://www.gutenberg.org/files/20203/20203-h/20203-h.htm#XVIII

Finally, we leave our discussion of Mr. Franklin with some quotes from his Poor Richard's Almanac of 1758.

Industry need not wish, and he that lives upon Hope will die fasting.

There are no Gains without Pains.

He that hath a Trade hath an Estate; and he that hath a Calling, hath an Office of Profit and Honor; but then the Trade must be worked at, and the Calling well followed, or neither the Estate nor the Office will enable us to pay our Taxes.

What though you have found no Treasure, nor has any rich Relation left you a Legacy, Diligence is the Mother of Good-luck, as Poor Richard says, and God gives all Things to Industry.

One To-day is worth two To-morrows, and farther, Have you somewhat to do To-morrow, do it To-day.

If you were a Servant, would you not be ashamed that a good Master should catch you idle? Are you then your own Master, be ashamed to catch yourself idle.

Stick to it steadily; and you will see great Effects, for Constant Dropping wears away Stones, and by Diligence and Patience the Mouse ate in two the Cable; and Little Strokes fell great Oaks.

Keep thy Shop, and thy Shop will keep thee; and again, If you would have your business done, go; if not, send.

If you would have a faithful Servant, and one that you like, serve yourself.[20] (From *Father Abraham's Speech*, forming the preface to Poor Richard's Almanac for 1758.)

---

[20] http://www.gutenberg.org/files/20203/20203-h/20203-h.htm#XVIII

Nathanael Greene

As long as the measures which conducted us safely through the first and most critical stages of the war shall be remembered with approbation; as long as the enterprises of Trenton and Princeton shall be regarded as the dawnings of that bright day which afterwards broke forth with such resplendent lustre; as long as the almost magic operations of the remainder of that remarkable winter, distinguished not more by these events than by the extraordinary spectacle of a powerful army straitened within narrow limits by the phantom of a military force, and never permitted to transgress those limits with impunity, in which skill supplied the place of means and disposition was the substitute for an army; as long, I say, as these operations shall continue to be the object of wonder, so long ought the name of Greene to be revered by a grateful country. To attribute to him a portion of the praise which is due as well to the formation as to the execution of the plans that effected these important ends can be no derogation from that wisdom and magnanimity which knew how to select and embrace counsels worthy of being pursued. (Alexander Hamilton)[21]

"We fight, get beaten, rise, and fight again." - Nathanael Greene

Date	Events
August 7, 1742	Born in Warwick, Rhode Island
1770	• Takes over the running of the family foundry in Coventry, Rhode Island • He may have been elected to the Rhode Island General Assembly
1774	Marries Catharine Littlefield Greene; they would have 5 children
October 1774	Organizes a militia group known as the Kentish Guards; Greene is expelled from the pacifist Quakers as a result. He also started teaching himself military tactics from books.
May 8, 1775	Becomes Major General of the Rhode Island Army of Observation

---

[21] *Nathanael Greene*, by George Washington Greene (Tichnor and Fields, 1866)

Date	Events
June 22, 1775	Promoted to brigadier general in the Continental Army by the Continental Congress
March 1776	Put in command by Washington of Boston
August 9, 1776	Promoted to major general and assigned command of troops on Long Island; designs fortifications near the Brooklyn Heights
October 1776	Placed in command of Fort Lee in New Jersey and Fort Washington (across the river from Fort Lee)
November 16, 1776	Howe defeats the Continental Army at the Battle of Fort Washington (Washington Heights, Manhattan)
December 25, 1776	Washington wins a stunning victory by crossing the Delaware River and capturing 900+ Hessian soldiers in Trenton – Greene commanded one of two columns
September 11, 1777	Greene in charge of the reserve corps at the Continental Army defeat at Brandywine, Pennsylvania
October 4, 1777	British defeat Washington at Germantown – Greene arrives late to the battle, but does engage the enemy
March 2, 1778	Appointed Quartermaster General of the Continental Army by Washington at Valley Forge
June 28, 1778	Commands the right wing at the Battle of Monmouth
August 29, 1778	With Lafayette, commands Continental Army at the Battle of Rhode Island (Aquidneck Island, Rhode Island). After a poorly coordinated joint action between the Americans and the French at Newport, the British keep control of Aquidneck Island.
August 1780	• Resigns as Quartermaster General after conflicts with the Continental Congress (Greene wanted to centralize; Congress wanted to provide supplies through the states) • British decisively defeat Horatio Gates near Camden, South Carolina
September 29, 1780	Presides over the court which condemned British spymaster Major John André to death
October 1780	Greene becomes commander at West Point, and builds up its defenses
October 5,	The Continental Congress decides to leave it up to

Date	Events
1780	Washington as to who should lead the Southern command; Washington chooses Greene
October 7, 1780	Continentals win a key battle at Kings Mountain (North Carolina) under Colonel William Campbell
December 2, 1780	Greene takes control of the Southern Command at Charlotte, North Carolina; he is to answer to no one but the Commander-in-Chief
January 17, 1781	Lopsided Continental Army victory under General Daniel Morgan at the Battle of Cowpens, South Carolina
March 15, 1781	Greene takes on Cornwallis at the Battle of Guilford Court House in North Carolina; Greene retreats, but Cornwallis is forced to retreat three days later towards Wilmington
Summer 1781	Greene recaptures most of South Carolina
September 8, 1781	Greene forces the British under Lieutenant Colonel Alexander Stewart to retreat to Charleston after the Battle of Eutaw Springs
December 14, 1782	The British abandon Charleston, South Carolina, which is quickly occupied by Green's forces
1785	Greene retires to his estate "Mulberry Grove", in Chatham County, Georgia
June 19, 1786	Dies of sunstroke on his estate near Savannah, Georgia
1808	Greensboro, North Carolina is named for Nathanael Greene
1936	1 cent stamp commemorating Greene, Washington and Mount Vernon is issued
December 19, 1964	USS Nathanael Greene nuclear submarine is commissioned (decommissioned 1986)

Nathanael Greene is often considered to be the best general in the Continental Army next to Washington himself. While an adequate Major General serving under Washington in 1776/78, his fame and acclaim rose when he took sole command of the Southern Command in 1780.

Prior to 1780, Greene served in several capacities in the Continental Army. Greene, a self-taught military strategist, was promoted from private to Major General of a militia unit in 1775. He would soon be promoted to one of four major generals under Washington. He distinguished himself at Brandywine, Germantown, Trenton and Monmouth, although he was less successful at the Battle of Fort Washington and the Battle of Rhode Island. In 1778, Washington appointed him as Quartermaster General of the Continental Army. He would hold the position for a little over two years, resigning because of disputes with the Continental Congress over how supplies should be distributed, and because he wanted to get back to the field.

On December 2, 1780, Greene was put in charge of the Southern Command by Washington. He had wide-ranging authority to conduct the Southern Command as he saw fit - he was to answer to no one but the Commander-in-Chief.

There were three significant battles in 1781 in the Southern Command. On January 17, 1781, General Daniel Morgan won a lopsided victory over the British at the Battle of Cowpens, South Carolina. On March 15, 1781, Greene fought Cornwallis at the Battle of Guilford Court House in North Carolina. While Greene made a tactical retreat from the battlefield, Cornwallis was forced to retreat three days later towards Wilmington. On September 8, 1781, Greene forced the British under Lieutenant Colonel Alexander Stewart to retreat to Charleston after the Battle of Eutaw Springs.

Greene is considered a brilliant strategist during his time as head of the Southern Command. He strategies are somewhat reminiscent of William Tecumseh Sherman's strategies during the North Georgia part of the Atlanta Campaign. Green didn't win a lot of battles, but through strategic retreats and flanking movements, he basically pushed Cornwallis out of the interior of the Carolinas and into the coastal cities. (Sherman didn't win many battles in North Georgia, either, but through flanking movements he inched ever closer to Atlanta.)

Nathanael Greene[22]

---

[22] http://www.archives.gov/research/military/american-revolution/pictures/images/revolutionary-war-080.jpg

Nathan Hale

Date	Events
June 6, 1755	Born in Coventry, Connecticut
1768	Attends Yale College; meets Benjamin Tallmadge
1773	Graduates with honors; teaches school at East Haddam and later in New London
1774	Holds a summer school for young ladies
1775	Joins a Connecticut militia as a first lieutenant, but does not participate in the Siege of Boston
July 4, 1775	Receives a letter from Benjamin Tallmadge encouraging him to greater efforts to the Patriot cause; as a result, he becomes a first lieutenant in the 7th Connecticut Regiment
Spring 1776	Stationed in Manhattan building fortifications at Bayard's Mount ("Bunker's Hill"), the steepest hill in southern Manhattan
July 1776	Major Robert Rogers is chartered by William Howe to form a guerrilla band, similar to such bands in the French and Indian War. Rogers begins trolling of the coast of Long Island for recruits.
August 27, 1776	British successfully invade Long Island
September 8, 1776	During British occupation of Battle of Long Island, Hale volunteers to spy on the British for Washington
September 12, 1776	Hale is ferried behind British lines (Huntington, Long Island, New York)
September 15, 1776	Southern Manhattan falls to the British, and Washington retreats to the Harlem Heights
September 21, 1776	Great New York Fire of 1776. No one knows who started it, but the British arrested 200 Colonial sympathizers. Hale is arrested on Long Island by Major Robert Rogers.
September 22, 1776 11:00 am	Hale is hung at what is today 66th Street and Third Avenue
1776	Fort Nathan Hale in New Haven is established
November 25, 1893	Statue erected in City Hall Park, New York
June 6, 1900	Nathan Hale Memorial Chapter Daughters of the

Date	Events
	American Revolution organized in East Haddam, CT
1912	Statue erected in front of Connecticut Hall at Yale. There are several copies of this statue extant, including at CIA headquarters in Langley, VA.
1925, 1929	Postal stamps commemorating Nathan Hale issued by the United States Postal Service
January 12, 1963	*USS Nathan Hale* (SSBN-623) nuclear submarine commissioned (decommissioned 1986)
1985	Designated the state hero of Connecticut
2000	Handwritten history of the American revolution written by Tory shopkeeper Consider Tiffany donated to the Library of Congress by G. Bradford Tiffany

Nathan Hale, born June 6, 1755 in Coventry, Connecticut, was one of the first spies in the Colonial army, and one of the first martyrs to the patriot cause. He will be forever remembered for his last words before being hung by the British - "I only regret that I have but one life to lose for my country."

He was only 21 when he died, and probably had never fired a gun in anger. After graduating from Yale in 1773, he began a short career teaching school, first at East Haddam and later in New London (both in Connecticut).

In 1775, he joined a Connecticut militia as a first lieutenant, but he did not participate in the Siege of Boston with his regiment. This may be because he was ambivalent at that stage of the game about fighting for the Colonials, or because of his teaching contract - we'll probably never know.

We do know that on July 4, 1775, he received a letter from Benjamin Tallmadge (a chum from Yale) encouraging him to greater efforts to the Patriot cause; as a result, he became a first lieutenant in the 7th Connecticut Regiment.

By the Spring of 1776, Hale was stationed in Manhattan building fortifications at Bayard's Mount ("Bunker's Hill"), the steepest hill in southern Manhattan. His unit did not participate in the Battle of Long Island on August 27, 1776.

On September 8, 1776, Hale answered a call for volunteers to spy for Washington on British-occupied Long Island. During this period, spying was considered to be a less than savory way to make a living, but Hale answered the call. On September 12, 1776, he was ferried behind British

lines to Huntington, Long Island, New York. His assignment: gather intelligence on the British preparations to invade Manhattan. His cover: an itinerant school teacher looking for work. (Photo: "Sculpture "Nathan Hale," exterior of Department of Justice, Constitution Ave., Washington, D.C."[23])

Three days later, on September 15, 1776, Southern Manhattan fell to the British, and Washington retreated north to the Harlem Heights. Thus, Hale's original *raison d'etre* for being on Long Island had disappeared. However, he stayed on, evidently trying to raise a small force of Colonial sympathizers on Long Island.

---

[23] Public domain. Library of Congress
http://www.loc.gov/pictures/item/2010720200/. Highsmith Archive.

It appears that Hale trusted in the wrong person. On September 21, 1776, he was arrested on Long Island by Major Robert Rogers, who had recently been chartered by General William Howe to form a guerrilla band, similar to such bands in the French and Indian War. Tory shopkeeper Consider Tiffany, who later wrote a handwritten history of the Revolutionary War, described Hale's arrest, in a manuscript now in the Library of Congress:

[Rogers] "detected several American officers, that were sent to Long Island as spies, especially Captain Hale, who was improved in disguise, to find whether the Long Island inhabitants were friends to America or not. Colonel Rogers having for some days, observed Captain Hale, and suspected that he was an enemy in disguise; and to convince himself, Rogers thought of trying the same method, he quickly altered his own habit, with which he Made Capt Hale a visit at his quarters, where the Colonel fell into some discourse concerning the war, intimating the trouble of his mind, in his being detained on an island, where the inhabitants sided with the Britains against the American Colonies, intimating withal, that he himself was upon the business of spying out the inclination of the people and motion of the British troops. This intrigue, not being suspected by the Capt, made him believe that he had found a good friend, and one that could be trusted with the secrecy of the business he was engaged in; and after the Colonel's drinking a health to the Congress: informs Rogers of the business and intent. The Colonel, finding out the truth of the matter, invited Captain Hale to dine with him the next day at his quarters, unto which he agreed. The time being come, Capt Hale repaired to the place agreed on, where he met his pretended friend, with three or four men of the same stamp, and after being refreshed, began the same conversation as hath been already mentioned. But in the height of their conversation, a company of soldiers surrounded the house, and by orders from the commander, seized Capt Hale in an instant. But denying his name, and the business he came upon, he was ordered to New York. But before he was carried far, several persons knew him and called him by name; upon this he was hanged as a spy, some say, without being brought before a court martial."[24]   (Consider Tiffany)

What happened next is not fully documented, but it appears that Hale was taken to Southern Manhattan where he was interviewed by General William Howe. Hale freely admitted who he was, and why he was on Long Island. Howe sentenced him to hang the next day.

By the end of the 19th century, Nathan Hale was the subject of plays[25]

Some accounts say that he spent the night in a local greenhouse, and was refused both a Bible and a priest. The next day, September 22, 1776 at 11:00 am, he was hung at

[24] Library of Congress http://www.loc.gov/loc/lcib/0307-8/hale.html
[25] Library of Congress http://www.loc.gov/pictures/item/2014637201/

what is today 66th Street and Third Avenue in Manhattan (Park of Artillery).

"Sketch of the country illustrating the late engagement in Long Island."[26]

---

[26] Library of Congress http://hdl.loc.gov/loc.gmd/g3802l.ar115000

So, how do we know that his last words were "I only regret that I have but one life to lose for my country"? A British officer named John Montresor was present at the hanging, and heard the words. He later passed along Hale's last words to an American officer named William Hull (later a general). It was Hull that publicized Hale's last word.

It wasn't until the early 19th century, though, that Hale's martyrdom became a *cause celebre*. Below is a typical description of Hale's final hours and final words.

> But while such happy thoughts were passing in his mind; while his heart beat high with the expectation of a speedy return to his fellow soldiers, and his friends; a sudden cloud dimmed the bright vision. Arrested by the hand of the enemy, he was already beyond the reach of mercy. His object discovered, he frankly confessed it. The die was cast. He was tried and convicted; and now he stands upon the scaffold. Let us pause, and for a moment contemplate the awful scene which is so soon to close. Calm, collected, firm— no servile fear of death is marked upon his brow. Conscious of no guilt, how dignified his deportment!—how undaunted his courage! As he looks around upon the assembled multitude, who are gathered together to behold his departure from the world, and sees before him none but his enemies, he neither hesitates nor falters; but with an undaunted look, resolved to die for his country, he yields to the sacrifice.
>
> As a dying request, he asks that a Bible may be furnished him. With a fiendish malice, this last dying prayer is refused; and his letters, which he desires may be conveyed to his mother and his friends, are destroyed. His last sad farewell they never will receive! Still firm amid all this cruelty, he utters no complaint; but as his eyes are turned for the last time toward the home of his birth, while a beam of patriotic fire kindles up his countenance, he exclaims: "*I only lament that I have but one life to lose for my country;*" and he dies, a martyr in the cause of liberty. Such was the fate of Hale.[27]

---

[27] *The Hesperian, Volume 2*, by William Davis Gallagher, Otway Curry (John D. Nichols, 1838)

So, young Nathan Hale wasn't a great fighter, or even a great spy. We revere him today because of his unerring devotion to the cause of the patriots.

Alexander Hamilton

Date	Events
January 11, 1755 or 1757	Born in the Leeward Islands of British West Indies
August 30, 1772	His essay on a recent hurricane is published in the *Royal Danish-American Gazette*
c. 1774	Begins attending King's College (Columbia University) in New York City
December 1774	Publishes *A Full Vindication of the Measures of Congress* anonymously, supporting the actions of the First Continental Congress
1775	Publishes *The Farmer Refuted*, a polemic against the loyalist views of Samuel Seabury
1776	Organizes an artillery unit, New York Provincial Company of Artillery, and is elected captain. They would fight at the Battle of White Plains and at the Battle of Trenton.
March 1, 1777	Becomes Washington's aide-de-camp with the rank of Lieutenant Colonel
December 14, 1780	Marries Elizabeth Schuyler. They would have 8 children.
July 31, 1781	At Hamilton's request, Hamilton is given a field command over a New York light infantry battalion
October 14, 1781	As commander of three battalions (400 men) at Yorktown, he launches a successful nighttime bayonet attack on Redoubt 10
July 1782	Appointed to the Congress of the Confederation
July 1783	Resigns from Congress and becomes a lawyer in New York
1784	Establishes the Bank of New York
September 11/14, 1786	Sponsors the *Meeting of Commissioners to Remedy Defects of the Federal Government* in Annapolis, Maryland, calling for a Constitutional Convention
1787/88	Writes 51 of 85 sections of the Federalist Papers
1787	New York State Legislature assemblyman (from New York County)
May 25, 1787 - September 17,	Member of the Constitutional Convention. He was the only New York representative to sign the new

Date	Events
1787	Constitution.
November 3, 1788 – March 2, 1789	Member of the Congress of the Confederation (from New York)
September 11, 1789 – January 31, 1795	First United States Secretary of the Treasury
1791	Named a Fellow of the American Academy of Arts and Sciences
January 14, 1790	*First Report on the Public Credit*, presented to the House of Representatives, proposed the Federal government taking over the debt of the states (passed July 26, 1790)
August 4, 1790	At Hamilton's urging, the *Revenue Cutter Service* is established, to combat smuggling and piracy of the coasts. It can be viewed as the beginning of the Coast Guard.
December 14, 1790	*Second Report on Public Credit* – proposed the creation of a National Bank (passed House February 8, 1791)
January 28, 1791	*Report on the Establishment of a Mint* resulted in the Coinage Act of 1792
December 5, 1791	*Report on Manufactures* calls for protectionist duties on imports
1791	Nine month affair with Maria Reynolds
1794	The Whiskey Rebellion in Western Pennsylvania is at least partly in response to excise taxes on whiskey and other spirits put into place by Hamilton
1795	• The Jay Treaty with England is signed, encouraging trade. Hamilton wrote the instructions for Jay to use when negotiating the treaty. • Resigns his cabinet position when an extra-marital affair comes to light
1798/99	Calls for war against France after the XYZ Affair
December 14, 1799 – June 15, 1800	Senior Officer of the United States Army (major general) during the Quasi-War with France
1800	Writes critical *Letter from Alexander Hamilton, Concerning the Public Conduct and Character of*

Date	Events
	John Adams, Esq. President of the United States
1801	Establishes the Federalist-leaning *New York Evening Post* (today known as the *New York Post*)
July 12, 1804	Dies in New York City, New York from a gunshot wound from Aaron Burr during a duel in Weehawken, New Jersey
1812	• Hamilton College established in New York • Fort Hamilton in Brooklyn established
1870	30 cent stamp honoring Hamilton issued by the United States Post Office
1928	Hamilton begins appearing on the $10 bill
March 19, 1956	United States Post Office issues a $5 stamp honoring Hamilton (*Liberty Issue*)
1957	3 cent "Alexander Hamilton Bicentennial" stamp issued
April 27, 1962	Hamilton Grange National Memorial established, now located in St. Nicholas Park in New York City

He was a war hero, a prolific writer, a major reason that we have two political parties today, a banker, a politician, the founder of the Coast Guard and the first Secretary of the Treasury. He was a foe of John Adams, even thought they were in the same political party.

As a war hero, he started out as a captain in an artillery regiment, but soon was promoted to Lieutenant Colonel, as he became Washington's aide-de-camp. After threatening to resign from the army, Washington gave him a field command over a New York light infantry battalion in July 1781. On October 14, 1781, as commander of three battalions (400 men) at Yorktown, he launched a successful nighttime bayonet attack on Redoubt 10. And to top off his military career, he was made Senior Officer of the United States Army (major general) in 1799/1800.

Below is an excerpt from a letter from Hamilton to Washington in May 1781 where he is setting the stage for being granted a field command (he'd served as Washington's aide-de-camp for most of the War.)

> It is distinguished by the circumstances I have before intimated; my early entrance into the service; my having made the campaign of '76, the most disagreeable of the war, at the head of a company of artillery, and having been entitled, in that corps, to a rank, equal in degree, more ancient in date, than I now possess; my having made all the subsequent campaigns in the family of the Commander-in-chief, in a constant course of important and laborious service. These are my pretensions, at this advanced period of the war, to being employed in the only way which my situation admits; and I imagine they would have their weight in the minds of the officers in general. I only urge them a second time, as reasons which will not suffer me to view the matter in the same light with your Excellency, or to regard, as impracticable, my appointment in a light corps, should there be one formed. I entreat they may be understood in this sense only. I am incapable of wishing to obtain any object by importunity. I assure your Excellency, that I am too well persuaded of your candor, to attribute your refusal to any other cause than an apprehension of inconveniences that may attend the appointment.[28] (Letter from Hamilton to Washington, May 2, 1781)

As a politician, he served as a New York State Legislature assemblyman, and served twice as a member of the Congress of the Confederation. He was a key player in the intrigues surrounding the 1796 and 1800 presidential and vice-presidential elections. As a member of the Constitutional Convention, he was the only New York representative to sign the new Constitution (which he had vigorously campaigned in favor of).

As noted above, Hamilton and John Adams were foes, even though they were both Federalists. Below is an excerpt from Hamilton's 1800 *Letter from Alexander Hamilton, Concerning the Public Conduct and Character of John Adams, Esq. President Of The United States*.

---

[28] *The Works of Alexander Hamilton*, by Alexander Hamilton (John F. Trow, 1850)

I was one of that numerous class who had conceived a high veneration for Mr. Adams, on account of the part he acted in the first stages of our revolution. My imagination had exalted him to a high eminence, as a man of patriotic, bold, profound, and comprehensive mind. But in the progress of the war, opinions were ascribed to him, which brought into question, with me, the solidity of his understanding. He was represented to be of the number of those who favored the enlistment of our troops annually, or for short periods, rather than for the term of the war; a blind and infatuated policy, directly contrary to the urgent recommendation of General Washington, and which had nearly proved the ruin of our cause. He was also said to have advocated the project of appointing yearly a new Commander of the Army; a project which, in any service, is likely to be attended with more evils than benefits; but which in ours, at the period in question, was chimerical, from the want of persons qualified to succeed, and pernicious, from the peculiar fitness of the officer first appointed, to strengthen, by personal influence, the too feeble cords which bound to the service, an ill-paid, ill-clothed, and undisciplined soldiery...

...Mr. Adams never could forgive the men who had been engaged in the plan; though it embraced some of his most partial admirers. He has discovered bitter animosity against several of them. Against me, his rage has been so vehement, as to have caused him more than once, to forget the decorum, which, in his situation, ought to have been an inviolable law. It will not appear an exaggeration to those who have studied his character, to suppose that he is capable of being alienated from a system to which he has been attached, because it is upheld by men whom he hates. How large a share this may have had in some recent aberrations, cannot easily be determined. [29]

---

[29] *Letter from Alexander Hamilton, Concerning the Public Conduct and Character of John Adams, Esq. President of the United States*, by Alexander Hamilton (Printed for John Lang by George F. Hopkins, 1800)

"A Hamilton from the original painting by Chappel"[30]

As a prolific and influential writer, he wrote tracts such as:

- *A Full Vindication of the Measures of Congress* (published anonymously), supported the actions of the First Continental Congress (December 1774)
- *The Farmer Refuted*, was a polemic against the loyalist views of Samuel Seabury (1775)
- *The Federalist Papers* (51 of 85 were written by Hamilton) (1787/88)
- *First Report on the Public Credit* was presented to the House of Representatives. It proposed the Federal

---

[30] Library of Congress http://www.loc.gov/pictures/item/2008676310/

government taking over the debt of the states. (January 14, 1790)

- *Second Report on Public Credit* – proposed the creation of a National Bank (December 14, 1790)
- *Report on the Establishment of a Mint* resulted in the Coinage Act of 1792 (January 28, 1791)
- *Report on Manufactures* called for protectionist duties on imports (December 5, 1791)
- *Letter from Alexander Hamilton, Concerning the Public Conduct and Character of John Adams, Esq. President of the United States* (1800)

As the first Secretary of State, Hamilton argued in favor of protectionism for American manufacturing and farmers, in the form of duties on imported goods. He pushed for the establishment of a mint, and for standardized coinage. He preferred centralized solutions to decentralized solutions, such as the Federal government taking on the War debts of individual states. And, for good measure, he established the *Revenue Cutter Service* to combat smuggling and piracy of the coasts. This can be viewed as the beginning of the Coast Guard.

Below is an excerpt from his 1791 *Report on Manufactures* where he calls for tariffs on imported gin and other spirits. In modern terms, Hamilton definitely would not have been a free-marketer.

The consumption of geneva, or gin, in this country is extensive. It is not long since distilleries of it have grown up among us to any importance. They are now becoming of consequence, but being still in their infancy, they require protection.

It is represented that the price of some of the materials is greater here than in Holland, from which place large quantities are brought; the price of labor considerably greater; capitals engaged in the business there much larger than those which are employed here; the rate of profits at which the undertakers can afford to carry it on much less; the prejudices in favor of importing gin strong. These circumstances are alleged to outweigh the charges which attend the bringing of the article from Europe to the United States and the present difference of duty, so as to obstruct the prosecution of the manufacture with due advantage.

Experiment could, perhaps, alone decide with certainty the justness of the suggestions which are made; but in relation to branches of manufacture so important, it would seem inexpedient to hazard an unfavorable issue, and better to err on the side of too great than of too small a difference in the particular in question.

It is, therefore, submitted, that an addition of two cents per gallon be made to the duty on imported spirits of the first class of proof, with a proportionable increase on those of higher proof; and that a deduction of one cent per gallon be made from the duty on spirits distilled within the United States, beginning with the first class of proof and a proportionable deduction from the duty on those of higher proof.[31]

[31] *Alexander Hamilton's Famous Report on Manufactures: Made to Congress In His Capacity as Secretary of the Treasury*, by Alexander Hamilton (Home Market Club, 1892)

John Hancock

Date	Events
1734	Reverend John Hancock baptizes John Adams
January 23, 1737	Born in Braintree (Quincy), Massachusetts, son of Reverend John Hancock
1750	Graduates from Boston Latin School
1754	Graduates from Harvard College
1760/61	While working for his uncle's import/export business, Hancock spends time living in Great Britain
October 1762	Becomes a member of the Masonic Lodge of St. Andrew in Boston
January 1763	Hancock becomes a full partner in his uncle's House of Hancock business
August 1764	Hancock inherits his uncle's business and belongings
1764	Sugar Act of 1764 passed
March 1765	Elected as a Boston selectmen
1765	Stamp Act passed
May 1766	Elected to Massachusetts House of Representatives
1767	Townshend Acts passed, putting new duties on imported goods, and improving customs enforcement
April 9, 1768	The British attempt to search Hancock's ship *Lydia*, but retreat when it turns out they have no search warrant
May 10, 1768	The British search his ship *Liberty* which may have been unloaded the night before
June 10, 1768	Customs officials seize the *Liberty*, after a search reveals smuggled goods
October 1768	Hancock is tried for smuggling, and defended by John Adams; the charges are dropped after a five month trial
March 1770	Boston Massacre; Hancock calls for the removal of British troops from Boston, which sort of happens – they are withdrawn to Castle William in Boston Harbor
April 1772	Hancock elected colonel of the *Boston Cadets* militia; one of their jobs was to protect the

Date	Events
	governor during public appearances (!)
1773	Hancock and Samuel Adams publish private letters of Governor Hutchinson that seem to advocate violence against the colonists
November 5, 1773	Hancock is the moderator of a Boston town meeting that votes that the Tea Act was an "Enemy to America"
December 16, 1773	Hancock speaks out against the Tea Act in a public meeting; the Boston Tea Party ensues (Hancock didn't participate)
March 5, 1774	Hancock delivers a speech at the fourth anniversary of the Boston Massacre, calling for British troops to leave Boston
May 1774	General Thomas Gage replaces Thomas Hutchinson as governor
June 17, 1774	The Massachusetts House sends five delegates to the First Continental Congress in Philadelphia; Hancock is not one of them
October 1774	Gage dissolves the Massachusetts legislature
October 7, 1774	The colonists form the Massachusetts Provincial Congress, with Hancock as president
December 1, 1774	The Provincial Congress elects Hancock as a delegate to the Second Continental Congress
April 1775	Fearing arrest, Samuel Adams and John Hancock retire to Hancock's childhood home in Lexington
April 18, 1775	Gage dispatches troops to Lexington and Concord; one of their objectives may have been to arrest Adams and Hancock.; Paul Revere warns Adams and Hancock
May 24, 1775 – October 31, 1777	President of the Continental Congress; chair of the Marine Committee
August 1, 1775	Marries Dorothy "Dolly" Quincy. They would have two children.
1776	• Appointed as senior major general of the Massachusetts militia • Hancock, Massachusetts incorporated
June 3, 1776	Frigate USS Hancock is launched
July 4, 1776	Declaration of Independence is approved by Congress. An August 2, 1776 copy was signed by

Date	Events
	John Hancock and other delegates, with Hancock's signature being in large, bold letters.
October 1777	Requests leave of absence from the Congress, and returns to Boston
December 1777	Re-elected to the Continental Congress, and to his position as moderator of the Boston town meeting
July 9, 1778	Hancock signs the Articles of Confederation, which is not ratified until 1781
August 1778	Leads 6,000 men in the French/Colonial attack on the British at Newport, Rhode Island (a British victory)
1780	Charter member of the American Academy of Arts and Sciences
October 25, 1780 – January 29, 1785	Governor of Massachusetts (wins 90% of the vote)
January 29, 1785	Resigns as governor, perhaps because of health reasons
1785	Elected as a delegate to the Confederation Congress (resigns 1786, perhaps because of ill health)
May 30, 1787 – October 8, 1793	Governor of Massachusetts
January 1788	Elected president of the Massachusetts ratifying convention. The Constitution would pass 187 to 168, after a speech from Hancock endorsing the new Constitution.
1789	Receives 4 electoral votes in the U. S. presidential election
October 8, 1793	Dies at Hancock Manor, Boston, Massachusetts. He is buried at the Granary Burying Ground.
1806	Hancock, New York established
October 26, 1850	Steam tug USS John Hancock launched
1896	A memorial is placed on Hancock's grave
November 8, 1902	Navy acquires transport ship USS Hancock (AP-3)
January 24, 1944	Essex-class aircraft carrier USS Hancock (CV-19) launched
October 29,	Destroyer USS John Hancock (DD-981) launched

Date	Events
1977	(scrapped 2007)

John Hancock was a merchant, politician, perhaps an occasional smuggler, and a soldier. He was, at the time of the Revolution, one of the richest men in the Colonies. He risked it all for American freedom.

"John Hancock's defiance: July 4th 1776"[32]

Hancock received his wealth from his Uncle Thomas, who both raised John and apprenticed him in his successful import/export business. In August 1764, Hancock inherited his uncle's business and belongings. Hancock immediately went to work to expand the business even more.

As a prominent citizen of Boston, and a successful merchant in Boston, Hancock was one of the people most negatively impacted by the various duties and taxes levied by the British overlords of Boston. He was outspoken in his condemnation

---

[32] Library of Congress http://www.loc.gov/pictures/item/2002707681/

both of the British duties and taxes, as well as their occupation of Boston. Hancock was involved in a first-hand basis in 1768 when two of his ships – the *Lydia* and the *Liberty* – were searched by the British for smuggled goods, and the latter ship was confiscated.

In October 1768, Hancock was tried for smuggling, and defended by John Adams; the charges were dropped after a five month trial.

To call one a smuggler in those days meant something different than today. Smuggling was a political act, used by many merchants as a way to avoid paying oppressive taxes and especially import duties on their goods.

Hancock had a limited but interesting military career. It began in April 1772 when Governor Hutchinson appointed Hancock as colonel of the Boston Cadets militia. One of the jobs of this militia was to protect the governor during public appearances. It is a little vague why Hutchinson, who had been greatly maligned by Hancock in public on several occasions, would put Hancock in charge of his protection service. Perhaps it was an attempt to co-opt Hancock to the side of the British.

After being turned down by George Washington for a commission in the Continental Army, in 1776, Hancock was appointed as senior major general of the Massachusetts militia. His big moment in the field was when he led 6,000 men in the French/Colonial attack on the British at Newport, Rhode Island. The attack was pushed back, and is considered a British victory.

Hancock also held many political positions during and after the American Revolution, including:

- Elected as a Boston selectmen (March 1765)
- Elected to Massachusetts House of Representatives (May 1766)
- Hancock is the moderator of a Boston town meeting that votes that the Tea Act was an "Enemy to America" (November 5, 1773)
- The colonists form the Massachusetts Provincial Congress, with Hancock as president (October 7, 1774)
- The Provincial Congress elects Hancock as a delegate to the Second Continental Congress (December 1, 1774)
- President of the Continental Congress; chair of the Marine Committee (May 24, 1775 – October 31, 1777)
- Re-elected to the Continental Congress, and to his position as moderator of the Boston town meeting (December 1777)
- Governor of Massachusetts (wins 90% of the vote) (October 25, 1780 – January 29, 1785)
- Elected as a delegate to the Confederation Congress (resigns 1786, perhaps because of ill health) (1785)
- Governor of Massachusetts (May 30, 1787 – October 8, 1793)
- Elected president of the Massachusetts ratifying convention. The Constitution would pass 187 to 168, after a speech from Hancock endorsing the new Constitution. (January 1788)
- Receives 4 electoral votes in the U. S. presidential election (1789)

One of the reasons that Hancock may not be as well-known as some of the Founding fathers is because he never wrote any books or pamphlets on political topics. We do have some letters written by Hancock though. Below are excerpts from three of them.

Two days after the passing of the Declaration of Independence (July 4, 1776), Hancock wrote a letter to George Washington notifying him as to the passage of the Declaration, and suggesting that Washington communicate the contents of the declaration to his army.

> The Congress, for some days past, have had their attention occupied by one of the most interesting and important subjects that could possibly come before them, or any other assembly of men.

> Although it is not possible to foresee consequences of human actions, yet it is, nevertheless, a duty we owe ourselves and posterity, in all our public counsels, to decide in the best manner we are able, and to trust the event to that Being, who controls both causes and events, to bring about his own determinations. Impressed with this sentiment, and at the same time fully convinced that our affairs may take a more favorable turn, the Congress have judged it necessary to dissolve all connections between Great Britain and the American Colonies, and to declare them free and independent States, as you will perceive by the enclosed Declaration, which **I am directed by Congress to transmit to you, and to request you will have proclaimed at the head of the army, in the way you shall think most proper**.[33] (July 6, 1776, to Washington; emphasis added.)

It is said that when signed copies of the Declaration were produced, John Hancock was first to affix his signature, saying, "I write so that George the Third may read without his spectacles." This story may, or may not be apocryphal.

In his letter to the "thirteen United States"of September 24, 1776, Hancock exhorted his compatriots to stand firm, even in the face of adversity:

> Let us convince our enemies that, as we are entered into the present contest for the defence of our liberties, so we are resolved, with the firmest reliance on Heaven for the justice of

---

[33] *John Hancock: His Book*, by Abram English Brown (Lee and Shepard Publishers, 1898)

our cause, never to relinquish it, but rather to perish in the ruins of it. If we do but remain firm, — if **we are not dismayed at the little shocks of fortune, and are determined, at all hazards, that we will be free**, — I am persuaded under the gracious smiles of Providence, assisted by our own most strenuous endeavors, we shall finally succeed, agreeably to our wishes, and thereby establish the independence, the happiness, and the glory of the United States of America.[34] (Letter to the "thirteen United States", Philadelphia, Sept. 24, 1776)

On October 25, 1780, John Hancock was sworn in as governor of Massachusetts. In his Inaugural Address, he spent a large portion of his speech discussing the need for supporting the Continental Army.

Gentlemen, Of all the weighty business that lies before you, a point of the first importance and most pressing necessity is the establishment of the army in such consistency and force, and with such seasonable and competent supplies, as may render it, in conjunction with the respectable forces sent to our assistance by our powerful and generous ally, an effectual defence to the free Constitutions and independence of the United States.

You cannot give too early or too serious an attention to that proportion of this business that falls to the share of this Commonwealth. The mode we have too long practised of re-enforcing the army by enlistments for a short time, has been found to be at once greatly ineffectual and extremely burthensome. The commander-in-chief, in whose abilities and integrity we justly repose the highest confidence, has repeatedly stated to us the great disadvantages arising from it; and the necessity of an army engaged for the whole war, and well provided, is now universally felt and acknowledged. Nor should a moment of time be lost in prosecuting every measure for establishing an object so essential to the preservation of our liberties and all that is dear to us. Care at the same time ought to be taken that the necessary supplies be committed to men on

---

[34] *John Hancock: His Book*, by Abram English Brown (Lee and Shepard Publishers, 1898)

whose principles and affection to our great cause, as well as capacity for such a service, we may safely depend.[35]

John Hancock risked everything for American freedom.

"John Hancock (1737-1793) Signer of the Declaration of Independence, President of the Continental Congress (1775-77), Governor of Mass. (1780-85)" Portrait by Jeremiah Meyer.[36]

[35] *John Hancock: His Book*, by Abram English Brown (Lee and Shepard Publishers, 1898)
[36] Public domain. Yale University Art Gallery.

Patrick Henry

Date	Events
May 29, 1736	Born in Hanover County, Virginia
1754	Marries Sarah Shelton, and receives a 300 acre farm, Pine Slash Farm, near Mechanicsville as a gift from his father-in-law. Henry and Sarah would have 6 children.
1760	Henry begins his law career
1764	Never really a going concern, the Henrys sell Pine Slash Farm; Henry works as a lawyer
1765	Henry was elected to the House of Burgesses from Louisa County
January 1765	Stamp Act passed
May 29, 1765	He introduces the radical Virginia Stamp Act Resolutions, stating that only the Virginia government could introduce new taxes, not Great Britain. When accused of treason, he replied, "If this be treason, make the most of it."
March 1773	Henry, with Thomas Jefferson and Richard Henry Lee led the House of Burgesses create a standing committee of correspondence. Such committees from the various states would eventually become the First Continental Congress.
1775	Sarah dies after a long mental illness; at one point in her illness, she is confined in a form of straight jacket
March 23, 1775	Henry gives a speech to the House of Burgesses that ends with the stirring rejoinder, "Is life so dear, or peace so sweet, as to be purchased at the price of chains and slavery? Forbid it, Almighty God! I know not what course others may take; but as for me, Give me Liberty, or give me Death!" The other delegates respond with cries of "To arms! To arms!"
April 20, 1775	Henry leads local militia against Lord Dunmore, the Royal Governor of the Colony of Virginia, when the latter attempts to remove gunpowder from a magazine in Williamsburg to a Royal Navy ship. The crisis ends when Lord Dunmore coughs up 330 pounds (the value of the powder), and leaves the

Date	Events
	colony.
August 1775	Colonel of the 1st Virginia Regiment
November 1775	Henry and James Madison elected as trustees of Hampden-Sydney College
July 5, 1776 – June 1, 1779	Governor of Virginia (term-limited)
September 1776	Fort Patrick Henry established near Kingsport, TN. It would serve as an outpost against the Cherokees during the Revolutionary War.
October 25, 1777	Marries Dorothea Dandridge. They would have 11 children (!) together.
1779	Purchases Leatherwood Plantation in Henry County, Virginia. The tobacco plantation is 10,000 acres. Henry owns 75 slaves.
1780/84	Member Virginia legislature
December 1, 1784 – December 1, 1786	Governor of Virginia
1788	Henry votes against the new Constitution at the Virginia convention because he is worried that the states will abrogate too much power in the Constitution . He strongly supported (and worked for) the Bill of Rights.
1789	Serves as an presidential elector from Campbell District
1794	Retires to Red Hill , a 520-acre plantation in Charlotte County
1795	Offered post of Secretary of State by George Washington, but declines
1798	Nominated by President John Adams as a special emissary to France, but declines because of health
June 6, 1799	Dies of stomach cancer in Brookneal, Virginia
April 17, 1861	CSS Patrick Henry commissioned by the Confederate States of America (the former Yorktown)
September 27, 1941	SS Patrick Henry Liberty ship launched (scrapped 1958)
1942/45	Camp Patrick Henry army base in Newport News, Virginia in operation
October 7,	U.S. Post Office issues a 1-dollar postage stamp

77

Date	Events
1955	honoring Patrick Henry
September 22, 1959	*USS Patrick Henry* (SSBN-599) nuclear submarine launched (scrapped 1997)
January 11, 1961	U.S. Post Office issues a 4-cent stamp in honor of Henry's "Give me liberty, or give me death" speech (*Credo* issue)
December 21, 1965	Scotchtown Plantation (Henry's from 1771/79) becomes a National Historic Landmark
October 15, 1966	Scotchtown Plantation (Henry's from 1771/79) added to the National Register of Historic Place
May 13, 1986	Red Hill Patrick Henry National Memorial

Patrick Henry was a lawyer, farmer/plantation owner, soldier, orator, and politician. He served as a member of the House of Burgesses of Virginia, served multiple terms as Governor of Virginia, both during and after the Revolutionary War, and served in the Virginia legislature from 1780/84.

It was during his time as a member of the House of Burgesses of Virginia that he gave one of the first rebuttals of the hated January 1765 Stamp Act with his introduction of the Virginia Stamp Act Resolution, which stated that only the Virginia colony government could introduce new taxes, not Great Britain. On May 29, 1765, during the debate over that Resolution, Henry made a key statement which was called treasonous at the time. William Wirt, an early biographer, describes that moment in the debates:

It was in the midst of this magnificent debate, while he was descanting on the tyranny of the obnoxious act, that he exclaimed in a voice of thunder, and with the look of a god "Cesar had his Brutus—Charles the First, his Cromwell and George the Third—('Treason!' cried the speaker—' Treason, treason!' echoed from every part of the house. It was one of those trying moments which is decisive of character. Henry faltered not for an instant; but rising to a loftier attitude, and fixing on the speaker an eye of the most determined fire, he finished his sentence with the firmest emphasis)—may profit by their example. If this be treason, make the most of it."[37]

This was one of the first shots fired in the American revolution, ten years before the shooting started.

"Patrick Henry before the Virginia House of Burgesses May 30, 1765"[38]

On March 23, 1775, Henry gave a speech to the House of Burgesses that cemented his place in patriot history. The speech ends with the stirring rejoinder, "Is life so dear, or peace so sweet, as to be purchased at the price of chains and slavery? Forbid it, Almighty God! I know not what course others may take; but as for me, Give me Liberty, or give me

---

[37] *Sketches of the Life and Character of Patrick Henry*, by William Wirt (Claxton, Kemsen & Haffelfinger, 1832)
[38] Library of Congress http://www.loc.gov/pictures/item/2006691555/

Death!" The other delegates responded with cries of "To arms! To arms!"

No man thinks more highly than I do of the patriotism, as well as abilities, of the very worthy gentlemen who have just addressed the house. But different men often see the same subject in different lights; and, therefore, I hope it will not be thought disrespectful to those gentlemen if, entertaining as I do opinions of a character very opposite to theirs, I shall speak forth my sentiments freely and without reserve. This is no time for ceremony. The question before the house is one of awful moment to this country. For my own part, I consider it as nothing less than a question of freedom or slavery; and in proportion to the magnitude of the subject ought to be the freedom of the debate. It is only in this way that we can hope to arrive at the truth, and fulfill the great responsibility which we hold to God and our country. Should I keep back my opinions at such a time, through fear of giving offense, I should consider myself as guilty of treason towards my country, and of an act of disloyalty toward the Majesty of Heaven, which I revere above all earthly kings.

Mr. President, it is natural to man to indulge in the illusions of hope. We are apt to shut our eyes against a painful truth, and listen to the song of that siren till she transforms us into beasts. Is this the part of wise men, engaged in a great and arduous struggle for liberty? Are we disposed to be of the numbers of those who, having eyes, see not, and, having ears, hear not, the things which so nearly concern their temporal salvation? For my part, whatever anguish of spirit it may cost, I am willing to know the whole truth, to know the worst, and to provide for it.

I have but one lamp by which my feet are guided, and that is the lamp of experience. I know of no way of judging of the future but by the past. And judging by the past, I wish to know what there has been in the conduct of the British ministry for the last ten years to justify those hopes with which gentlemen have been pleased to solace themselves and the House. Is it that insidious smile with which our petition has been lately received?

Trust it not, sir; it will prove a snare to your feet. Suffer not yourselves to be betrayed with a kiss. Ask yourselves how this gracious reception of our petition comports with those warlike preparations which cover our waters and darken our land. Are fleets and armies necessary to a work of love and reconciliation? Have we shown ourselves so unwilling to be reconciled that force must be called in to win back our love? Let us not deceive ourselves, sir. These are the implements of war and subjugation; the last arguments to which kings resort. I ask gentlemen, sir, what means this martial array, if its purpose be not to force us to submission? Can gentlemen assign any other possible motive for it? Has Great Britain any enemy, in this quarter of the world, to call for all this accumulation of navies and armies? No, sir, she has none. They are meant for us: they can be meant for no other. They are sent over to bind and rivet upon us those chains which the British ministry have been so long forging. And what have we to oppose to them? Shall we try argument? Sir, we have been trying that for the last ten years. Have we anything new to offer upon the subject? Nothing. We have held the subject up in every light of which it is capable; but it has been all in vain. Shall we resort to entreaty and humble supplication? What terms shall we find which have not been already exhausted? Let us not, I beseech you, sir, deceive ourselves. Sir, we have done everything that could be done to avert the storm which is now coming on. We have petitioned; we have remonstrated; we have supplicated; we have prostrated ourselves before the throne, and have implored its interposition to arrest the tyrannical hands of the ministry and Parliament. Our petitions have been slighted; our remonstrances have produced additional violence and insult; our supplications have been disregarded; and we have been spurned, with contempt, from the foot of the throne! In vain, after these things, may we indulge the fond hope of peace and reconciliation.

There is no longer any room for hope. If we wish to be free--if we mean to preserve inviolate those inestimable privileges for which we have been so long contending--if we mean not basely to abandon the noble struggle in which we have been so long engaged, and which we have pledged ourselves never to abandon until the glorious object of our contest shall be obtained--we must fight! I repeat it, sir, we must fight! An appeal to arms and to the God of hosts is all that is left us! They tell us, sir, that we are weak; unable to cope with so formidable an adversary. But when shall we be stronger? Will it be the next week, or the next year? Will it be when we are totally disarmed, and when a British guard shall be stationed in every house? Shall we gather strength by irresolution and inaction? Shall we acquire the means of effectual resistance by lying supinely on our backs and hugging the delusive phantom of hope, until our enemies shall have bound us hand and foot? Sir, we are not weak if we make a proper use of those means which the God of nature hath placed in our power. The millions of people, armed in the holy cause of liberty, and in such a country as that which we possess, are invincible by any force which our enemy can send against us. Besides, sir, we shall not fight our battles alone. There is a just God who presides over the destinies of nations, and who will raise up friends to fight our battles for us. The battle, sir, is not to the strong alone; it is to the vigilant, the active, the brave. Besides, sir, we have no election. If we were base enough to desire it, it is now too late to retire from the contest. There is no retreat but in submission and slavery! Our chains are forged! Their clanking may be heard on the plains of Boston! The war is inevitable--and let it come! I repeat it, sir, let it come.

It is in vain, sir, to extenuate the matter. Gentlemen may cry, Peace, Peace--but there is no peace. The war is actually begun! The next gale that sweeps from the north will bring to our ears the clash of resounding arms! Our brethren are already in the field! Why stand we here idle? What is it that gentlemen wish? What would they have? Is life so dear, or peace so sweet, as to be purchased at the price of chains and slavery? Forbid it, Almighty God! I know not what course others may take; but as for me, give me liberty or give me death![39] (Patrick Henry, March 23, 1775)

---

[39] http://www.law.ou.edu/ushistory/henry.shtml

"By the lion & unicorn, dieu & mon droit...", from a 1775 broadside[40]

Henry also took one of the first militia actions during the American Revolution on April 20, 1775 when he led the local militia against Lord Dunmore, the Royal Governor of the Colony of Virginia. Dunmore had conspired to remove gunpowder from a magazine in Williamsburg to a Royal Navy ship. The crisis ends when Lord Dunmore paid 330 pounds (the value of the powder), and left the colony.

In additional to several ships, and many schools in the United States named after him, counties in Virginia, Kentucky, Georgia, Ohio, Tennessee, Alabama, Illinois, and Missouri are named in his owner. He also has had two stamps released in his honor by the United States Post Office.

---

[40] Library of Congress   http://www.loc.gov/pictures/item/2007681477/

Thomas Jefferson

Date	Events
April 13, 1743	Born in Shadwell, Virginia
1757	Jefferson inherits 5,000 acres, including the land where Monticello would be built
1762	Graduates from the College of William & Mary (Williamsburg, VA)
1767	Admitted to Virginia bar
1768	Begins construction on Monticello (*Little Mountain*)
1769/75	Represents Albemarle County in the Virginia House of Burgesses
1769	Jefferson fails to pass legislation that would allow for owners to emancipate their slaves without permission of the governor
January 1, 1772	Marries third cousin Martha Wayles Skelton. They would have six children.
1774	• Writes *The Day of Fasting and Prayer* resolution in response to the British *Intolerable Act* • Writes *A Summary View of the Rights of British America,* suggesting that people should be able to govern themselves
1775/76	Delegate to the Second Continental Congress
1776	Primary author of the Declaration of Independence, which is written in 17 days
September 1776	Elected to Virginia House of Delegates
1777	Drafts *An Act of Establishing Religious Freedom*, which was ratified by the Virginia legislature in 1786
June 1, 1779 – June 3, 1781	Governor of Virginia
1780	Moves state capitol from Williamsburg to Richmond
June 1781	A kidnap plot against Jefferson headed by Banastre Tarleton is foiled when Jefferson is warned, and leaves Monticello
September 6, 1782	Mary Jefferson dies, probably from the after effects of childbirth
April 23, 1784	Authors *Land Ordinance of 1784*, in which Virginia ceded control of land northwest of the Ohio River

Date	Events
November 3, 1783 – May 7, 1784	Delegate to the Congress of the Confederation from Virginia
May 17, 1785 – September 26, 1789	United States Minister to France
1785	Writes *Notes on the State of Virginia* at the request of French diplomat François Barbé-Marbois
1787	• The *Northwest Ordinance of 1787* which would eventually create the states of Ohio, Indiana, Illinois, Michigan, Wisconsin and Minnesota is passed. Slavery was prohibited in the territories (and ensuing states), based on the *Jefferson Proviso*. • Fellow of the American Academy of Arts and Sciences
March 22, 1790 – December 31, 1793	Secretary of State
June 20, 1790	Jefferson, Hamilton and Madison come to agreement over a dinner that 1) the federal government would assume state's debt (Hamilton) and 2) the new national capitol would be on the Potomac River, not in New York or Philadelphia (Jefferson)
1791	Founds (with James Madison) Democratic-Republican Party
May 23, 1792	Writes a letter to Washington establishing what will later be basic tenets of the Democratic Party
1793	Jefferson supports France when England and France go to war. Jefferson would also generally support the French Revolution.
March 3, 1797	Elected president of the American Philosophical Society
March 4, 1797 – March 4, 1801	Vice President of the United States
1798/99	Drafts (with James Madison) the *Kentucky and Virginia Resolutions*, which opposed the *Alien and*

Date	Events
	Sedition Act of John Adams. Jefferson champions states rights over Federal rights.
February 17, 1801	After Aaron Burr and Jefferson received the same amount of votes in the presidential/vice-presidential race, the House of representatives elects Jefferson president (after 36 ballots)
March 4, 1801 – March 4, 1809	President of the United States. Jefferson would eliminate many of the federal taxes that Alexander Hamilton had put into place.
10 May 1801 – 10 June 1805	The United States defeats the Barbary Coast pirates after Jefferson sends in the U.S. Navy
1802	• Journalist James T. Callender, who had been turned down for a job as postmaster by Jefferson, claims that Jefferson had kept his slave Sally Hemings as a concubine • In a letter to the Danbury Baptists, Jefferson mentions "separation of church and state"
July 4, 1802	The United States Military Academy at West Point opens
March 1, 1803	Ohio becomes a state
July 4, 1803	Louisiana Purchase from Napoleon, for $15,000,000
1804/06	Jefferson authorizes the Lewis and Clarke Expedition
1807	• *Act Prohibiting Importation of Slaves* passed • *Embargo Act of 1807* made it illegal to export any items from the United States
1819	Founds the University of Virginia
c. 1819	Completes *The Life and Morals of Jesus of Nazareth* (sometimes called the *Jefferson Bible*)
November 4, 1824	Lafayette visits Jefferson at Monticello
July 4, 1826	Dies in Charlottesville, Virginia (the same day as John Adams)
1856	Jefferson 5¢ stamp issue
1862/1966,	Jefferson on the $2 bill issue
1861	Jefferson 5¢ stamp issue
1870	Jefferson 10¢ stamp issue
1890	Jefferson 30¢ stamp issue
1894	Jefferson 50¢ stamp issue

Date	Events
1903	Jefferson 50¢ stamp issue
1904	Jefferson/Louisiana Purchase stamp 2¢
1923	Jefferson 9¢ stamp issue
1938	• Jefferson on the nickel • Jefferson 3¢ stamp issue
1941	Carving of Washington, Lincoln, Jefferson and Theodore Roosevelt completed on Mt. Rushmore
April 13, 1943	Jefferson memorial in Washington, D.C. Is dedicated
1954	Jefferson 2¢ stamp issue
1976/present	Jefferson on the $2 bill
December 19, 1960	Monticello designated U.S. National Historic Landmark
October 15, 1966	Monticello placed on the National Register of Historic Places
1968	Jefferson 1¢ stamp issue
November 12, 1969	Poplar Forest (near Lynchburg) placed on the National Register of Historic Places
November 11, 1971	Poplar Forest (near Lynchburg) designated U.S. National Historic Landmark
1986	AMERIPEX stamp issue with Jefferson, 22¢
1987	Monticello and the University of Virginia in Charlottesville designated UNESCO World Heritage Site
1998	DNA tests showed that Sally Hemings' children likely came from a Jefferson, although not necessarily Thomas (he had a brother and five sons)

Thomas Jefferson was a plantation owner, lawyer, politician, political philosopher, author, inventor, revolutionary and patriot. He (along with James Madison) created the political party Democrat-Republican, which many view as the beginnings of the modern day Democrat party.

As a **politician**, Jefferson served many posts, including:

• Represented Albemarle County in the Virginia House of Burgesses (1769/75)

- Delegate to the Second Continental Congress (1775/76)
- Elected to Virginia House of Delegates (September 1776)
- Governor of Virginia (June 1, 1779 – June 3, 1781)
- Delegate to the Congress of the Confederation from Virginia (November 3, 1783 – May 7, 1784)
- Secretary of State (March 22, 1790 – December 31, 1793)
- Vice President of the United States (March 4, 1797 – March 4, 1801)
- President of the United States (March 4, 1801 – March 4, 1809)

THOMAS JEFFERSON,
3ᵈ PRESIDENT OF THE UNITED STATES.

"Thomas Jefferson, 3rd President of the United States", c. 1846[41]

[41] Library of Congress http://www.loc.gov/pictures/item/2009631979/

As **President**, Jefferson would eliminate many of the federal taxes that Alexander Hamilton had put into place. Other actions during his administration include:

- The United States defeats the Barbary Coast pirates after Jefferson sends in the U.S. Navy (10 May 1801 – 10 June 1805)
- The United States Military Academy at West Point opens (July 4, 1802)
- Ohio becomes a state (March 1, 1803)
- Louisiana Purchase from Napoleon, for $15,000,000 (July 4, 1803)
- Jefferson authorizes the Lewis and Clarke Expedition (1804/06)
- Act Prohibiting Importation of Slaves passed (1807)
- Embargo Act of 1807 made it illegal to export any items from the United States

Jefferson was pro states rights, against a centralized government, for decentralized taxation, and a staunch defender of religious freedom. He was against a standing army and navy, until forced to change his mind by the Barbary Coast pirates. His main ally during his time as president and vice-president was James Madison, and his primary adversaries were federalists John Adams and Alexander Hamilton.

As a **diplomat**, Jefferson served as United States Minister to France from May 17, 1785 – September 26, 1789. He always remained partial to France, especially when vis-a-vis Great Britain. He largely supported the French Revolution, which borrowed some of Jefferson's political philosophy.

As a **political philosopher**, Jefferson was the primary author of the Declaration of Independence, which was ratified on July 4, 1776. His 1774 *A Summary View of the Rights of British America* was one of the most radical documents of the time, suggesting that people had the right to self-governance.

"Writing the Declaration of Independence, 1776", c. 1932, shows (l to r) Franklin, Adams and Jefferson[42]

As an author, Jefferson wrote numerous bills and political tracts, and dabbled in religion and philosophy. Some of his works include:

- *The Day of Fasting and Prayer* resolution (1774), which was written in response to the British Intolerable Acts

---

[42] Library of Congress http://www.loc.gov/pictures/item/2002719535/

- *A Summary View of the Rights of British America* (1777) suggests that people should be able to govern themselves
- *An Act of Establishing Religious Freedom* is ratified by the Virginia legislature in 1786
- *Land Ordinance of 1784* results in Virginia ceding control of land northwest of the Ohio River (April 23, 1784)
- *Notes on the State of Virginia* (1785) was written at the request of French diplomat François Barbé-Marbois
- *The Life and Morals of Jesus of Nazareth* (c. 1819) (sometimes called the Jefferson Bible)

Jefferson was an **inventor** of some note (although not on the level of Benjamin Franklin. Some of his inventions included "The Great Clock", powered by the earth's gravitational pull, a cipher wheel, the polygraph, a device the made a copy of anything you wrote, and a pedometer, which measured the amount of steps one had taken.

But his greatest impact as an inventor was his effort to standardized firearms parts during his presidency.

Jefferson was a revolutionary and patriot. He is considered one of the Founding fathers of America.

"Jefferson Memorial, aerial view, Washington, D.C."[43]

There have really only been a couple of blemishes against his reputation over the years. The first involved when he was the Governor of Virginia. In June 1781, Cornwallis hatched a kidnap plot against Jefferson, which was headed by Banastre Tarleton. Virginia militia member Jack Jouett warned Jefferson ahead of time, and Jefferson escaped Monticello to a plantation that he owned to the west (Poplar Forest, near Lynchburg). Since Jefferson's term as governor ended the same month, he decided to just stay at Poplar Forest, and he made no attempt to contact the legislature again. He did not get reelected.

The second blemish, of course, concerns Sally Heming. As early as 1802, a journalist named James T. Callender, who had been turned down for a job as postmaster by Jefferson, claimed that Jefferson had kept his slave Sally Hemings as a concubine. In 1998, after a set of DNA tests were performed, it was proven that someone in the Jefferson line was the parent of at least one of Hemings' children. However, Thomas

---

[43] Public domain. Library of Congress.
http://www.loc.gov/pictures/item/2010630677/ Hightower collection.

Jefferson had a brother and five sons, so the evidence was not conclusive.

The charges regarding Jefferson and Sally Heming play into concerns about Jefferson's ambiguous stand on slavery. While he several times promoted anti-slavery legislation, he also personally kept close to 200 slaves himself.

Jefferson is most famous for writing the Declaration of Independence, so here it is in its entirety.

The Declaration of Independence: A Transcription

IN CONGRESS, July 4, 1776.

The unanimous Declaration of the thirteen united States of America,

When in the Course of human events, it becomes necessary for one people to dissolve the political bands which have connected them with another, and to assume among the powers of the earth, the separate and equal station to which the Laws of Nature and of Nature's God entitle them, a decent respect to the opinions of mankind requires that they should declare the causes which impel them to the separation.

We hold these truths to be self-evident, that all men are created equal, that they are endowed by their Creator with certain unalienable Rights, that among these are Life, Liberty and the pursuit of Happiness.--That to secure these rights, Governments are instituted among Men, deriving their just powers from the consent of the governed, --That whenever any Form of Government becomes destructive of these ends, it is the Right of the People to alter or to abolish it, and to institute new Government, laying its foundation on such principles and organizing its powers in such form, as to them shall seem most likely to effect their Safety and Happiness. Prudence, indeed, will dictate that Governments long established should not be changed for light and transient causes; and accordingly all experience hath shewn, that mankind are more disposed to suffer, while evils are sufferable, than to right themselves by abolishing the forms to which they are accustomed. But when a long train of abuses and usurpations, pursuing invariably the same Object evinces a design to reduce them under absolute Despotism, it is their right, it is their duty, to throw off such Government, and to provide new Guards for their future security.--Such has been the patient sufferance of these Colonies; and such is now the necessity which constrains them to alter their former Systems of Government. The history of the present King of Great Britain is a history of repeated injuries and usurpations, all having in direct object the establishment of an absolute Tyranny over these States. To prove this, let Facts be submitted to a candid world.

He has refused his Assent to Laws, the most wholesome and necessary for the public good.

He has forbidden his Governors to pass Laws of immediate and pressing importance, unless suspended in their operation till his Assent should be obtained; and when so suspended, he has utterly neglected to attend to them.

He has refused to pass other Laws for the accommodation of large districts of people, unless those people would relinquish the right of Representation in the Legislature, a right inestimable to them and formidable to tyrants only.

He has called together legislative bodies at places unusual, uncomfortable, and distant from the depository of their public Records, for the sole purpose of fatiguing them into compliance with his measures.

He has dissolved Representative Houses repeatedly, for opposing with manly firmness his invasions on the rights of the people.

He has refused for a long time, after such dissolutions, to cause others to be elected; whereby the Legislative powers, incapable of Annihilation, have returned to the People at large for their exercise; the State remaining in the mean time exposed to all the dangers of invasion from without, and convulsions within.

He has endeavoured to prevent the population of these States; for that purpose obstructing the Laws for Naturalization of Foreigners; refusing to pass others to encourage their migrations hither, and raising the conditions of new Appropriations of Lands.

He has obstructed the Administration of Justice, by refusing his Assent to Laws for establishing Judiciary powers.

He has made Judges dependent on his Will alone, for the tenure of their offices, and the amount and payment of their salaries.

He has erected a multitude of New Offices, and sent hither swarms of Officers to harrass our people, and eat out their substance.

He has kept among us, in times of peace, Standing Armies without the Consent of our legislatures.

He has affected to render the Military independent of and superior to the Civil power.

He has combined with others to subject us to a jurisdiction foreign to our constitution, and unacknowledged by our laws; giving his Assent to their Acts of pretended Legislation:

For Quartering large bodies of armed troops among us:

For protecting them, by a mock Trial, from punishment for any Murders which they should commit on the Inhabitants of these States:

For cutting off our Trade with all parts of the world:

For imposing Taxes on us without our Consent:

For depriving us in many cases, of the benefits of Trial by Jury:

For transporting us beyond Seas to be tried for pretended offences

For abolishing the free System of English Laws in a neighbouring Province, establishing therein an Arbitrary government, and enlarging its Boundaries so as to render it at once an example and fit instrument for introducing the same absolute rule into these Colonies:

For taking away our Charters, abolishing our most valuable Laws, and altering fundamentally the Forms of our Governments:

For suspending our own Legislatures, and declaring themselves invested with power to legislate for us in all cases whatsoever.

He has abdicated Government here, by declaring us out of his Protection and waging War against us.

He has plundered our seas, ravaged our Coasts, burnt our towns, and destroyed the lives of our people.

He is at this time transporting large Armies of foreign Mercenaries to compleat the works of death, desolation and tyranny, already begun with circumstances of Cruelty & perfidy scarcely paralleled in the most barbarous ages, and totally unworthy the Head of a civilized nation.

He has constrained our fellow Citizens taken Captive on the high Seas to bear Arms against their Country, to become the executioners of their friends and Brethren, or to fall themselves by their Hands.

He has excited domestic insurrections amongst us, and has endeavoured to bring on the inhabitants of our frontiers, the merciless Indian Savages, whose known rule of warfare, is an undistinguished destruction of all ages, sexes and conditions.

In every stage of these Oppressions We have Petitioned for Redress in the most humble terms: Our repeated Petitions have been answered only by repeated injury. A Prince whose character is thus marked by every act which may define a Tyrant, is unfit to be the ruler of a free people.

Nor have We been wanting in attentions to our Brittish brethren. We have warned them from time to time of attempts by their legislature to extend an unwarrantable jurisdiction over us. We have reminded them of the circumstances of our emigration and settlement here. We have appealed to their native justice and magnanimity, and we have conjured them by the ties of our common kindred to disavow these usurpations, which, would inevitably interrupt our connections and correspondence. They too have been deaf to the voice of justice and of consanguinity. We must, therefore, acquiesce in the necessity, which denounces our Separation, and hold them, as we hold the rest of mankind, Enemies in War, in Peace Friends.

We, therefore, the Representatives of the united States of America, in General Congress, Assembled, appealing to the Supreme Judge of the world for the rectitude of our intentions, do, in the Name, and by Authority of the good People of these Colonies, solemnly publish and declare, That these United Colonies are, and of Right ought to be Free and Independent States; that they are Absolved from all Allegiance to the British Crown, and that all political connection between them and the State of Great Britain, is and ought to be totally dissolved; and that as Free and Independent States, they have full Power to levy War, conclude Peace, contract Alliances, establish Commerce, and to do all other Acts and Things which Independent States may of right do. And for the support of this Declaration, with a firm reliance on the protection of divine Providence, we mutually pledge to each other our Lives, our Fortunes and our sacred Honor.[44]

---

[44] http://www.archives.gov/exhibits/charters/declaration_transcript.html

96

John Paul Jones

> The American squadron which sailed from Brest about the 15th July, under the command of Paul Jones, consists of one frigate of 40 guns, mounted on one deck, two 32 gun frigates, two Salem privateers of 18 and 20 guns, and a tender of 10 guns. The purpose of this squadron is to intercept the victuallers from Cork for North America. They have already taken two provision ships to New York, several trading vessels, and have much alarmed the coasts of Ireland.[45] (*London Chronicle* September 13, 1779)

Date	Events
July 6, 1747	Born John Paul in Kirkcudbrightshire, Scotland
1760	Sails as an apprentice aboard the *Friendship* out of Whitehaven, Cumberland County
1764	Sails on the *King George* as third mate
1766	Sails on the *Two Friends* as first mate
1768	Abandons the *Two Friends* in Jamaica in protest of the slave trade
1768	Sails in the brig *John*, and eventually is made captain when the captain and mate die of yellow fever
1770	• A ship's carpenter that Jones flogged dies several weeks later; Jones is arrested, but released on bail • Captain of the 22 gun *Betsy*, which sails the Britain, West Indies, America route
1771	Kills a man with a sword over a dispute over wages, and flees to Fredericksburg, Virginia (where his brother had recently died). Assumes the name John Paul Jones.
December 7, 1775	Appointed 1st Lieutenant of the Continental Navy on the 24-gun frigate *Alfred*
February 1776	Hoists the first U.S. ensign over a naval vessel (the *Alfred* on the Delaware River)
1776	Commands the sloop *Providence*, and captures 16 prizes along the coast of Nova Scotia
November 1, 1776	In command of the *Alfred*, the British cargo ship *Mellish* is captured

---

[45] *Life and Correspondence of John Paul Jones*, by John Paul Jones, Janette Taylor (A. Chandler, 1830)

Date	Events
June 14, 1777	Assigned command of the *USS Ranger*
November 1, 1777	Sails for France on the *Ranger*, where he will meet with Benjamin Franklin, John Adams
1778	With Benjamin Franklin, joins the Masonic Lodge *Les Neuf Sœurs* (*The Nine Sisters*)
February 6, 1778	France and America sign the Treaty of Alliance
February 14, 1778	The *USS Ranger* receives first salute from a French ship – a nine-gun salute fired from Captain Lamotte-Piquet's flagship
April 10, 1778	Leaves from Brest, France on the *Ranger* for Britain, where the *Ranger* attacks British shipping in the Irish Sea
April 17, 1778	Unsuccessful assault on Whitehaven, Cumbria, England
April 21, 1778	Unsuccessful midnight attack on the *HMS Drake* at Carrickfergus, Ireland (a drunk sailor lowered the anchor too soon)
April 23, 1778	Amphibious attack on Whitehaven; the guns of the town were spiked and some small fires were started
April 23/24, 1778	Attacks the Earl of Selkirk's manor on St Mary's Isle near Kirkcudbright. The Earl wasn't there, but some looting and pillaging was done. Jones would later personally buy the silver plate that was plundered, and return it to the Earl and his wife.
April 24, 1778	Captures the *HMS Drake* after an hour-long fight. He turns the prize over to his Lieutenant Simpson, who returns to France by another route than Jones. Jones later court-martials Simpson, for reasons that are obscure today.
1779	Takes command of the 42-gun *Bonhomme Richard*, a gift to America from French shipping magnate, Jacques-Donatien Le Ray
August 14, 1779	Provides an Irish diversion with a five ship squadron while French and Spanish ships head to England; Jones continues around the coast of Scotland into the North Sea
September 23, 1779	Jones' squadron approaches a British merchant fleet (41 ships) off of Flamborough Head, East Yorkshire, but the 50-gun *HMS Serapis* and the 22-gun

Date	Events
	Countess of Scarborough intervene
September 23, 1779 7:00 p.m.	Battle of Flamborough Head. Jones tries to lock the *Bonhomme Richard* and the *Serapis* together, knowing he is outgunned. When asked to surrender by the *Serapis*, Jones replies "I have not yet begun to fight!" With the help of the 36-gun *Alliance* and the 32-gun *Pallas*, the *Serapis* and *Countess of Scarborough* eventually surrender. The *Bonhomme Richard* doesn't survive the attack, but Jones and most of the crew do, taking over the *Serapis*.
1780	King of France Louis XVI bestows Jones with the title "Chevalier", and a membership in the *l'Institution du Mérite Militaire*
1787	The Continental Congress creates a medal of gold in commemoration of his "valor and brilliant services"
April 23, 1787	Goes to work for Empress Catherine II of Russia as a rear admiral; he would be pressed into naval operations against the Turks
June 8, 1788	Awarded the Order of St. Anne
April 1789	Jones is arrested on the word of rivals for raping a 12-year old girl, but the charges are soon dropped
June 1792	Named U.S. Consul to the Dey of Algiers
July 18, 1792	Dies in Paris, France of interstitial nephritis. He is buried in Saint Louis Cemetery for Alien Protestants
April 7, 1905	The body of Jones is dug up in Paris. It would be brought to the United States on the *USS Brooklyn*, with an escort of three other cruisers. Seven battleships would join the convoy along the way.
April 24, 1906	After a speech by Theodore Roosevelt, Jones' coffin is placed in Bancroft Hall at the United States Naval Academy, Annapolis, Maryland
January 26, 1913	Remains are re-interred at the Naval Academy Chapel in Annapolis
1937	1¢ stamp honoring John Paul Jones issued by the Post Office
May 7, 1955	Destroyer *USS John Paul Jones* (DD-932) launched (decommissioned 1982)
October 26, 1991	Guided missile destroyer *USS John Paul Jones* (DDG-53) launched
1959	Portrayed by Robert Stack in the movie *John Paul*

Date	Events
	Jones

He was a man of the sea from age 13 until the time he died. He had, what we might call today, an anger management problem. He fled to America in 1771 after killing a man in a dispute over wages, and added "Jones" to his name "John Paul". He was accused of acting like a pirate even when flying under the flag of the United States. It sometimes seemed like he was a bit of a glory seeker. He  didn't play well with his superiors. He sometimes battled with peers. (Photo: "John Paul Jones, commodore au service des Etats-Unis de l'Amérique"[46])

And yet, he was pretty much the only person who took the American Revolution to the British Isles, and gave them a taste of what the war was about. His forays in the Irish and North Seas in 1777/78 were the first significant victories of the U.S. Navy. As such, he is sometimes referred to as the "Father of the United States Navy".

His two greatest victories included the capture of the sloop o' war *HMS Drake* on April 24, 1778 off of Carrickfergus, Ireland, and the epic Battle of Flamborough Head on September 23, 1779, off the coast of northeast England. Jones lost his ship, the *Bonhomme Richard*, but captured the 50-gun *HMS Serapis*, and became immortal when he answered a surrender request with the line "I have not yet begun to fight!"

---

[46] Library of Congress http://www.loc.gov/pictures/item/2003689054/

The capture of the HMS Drake is described below, in Jones' own words.

On the morning of the 24th, I was again off Carrickfergus, and would have gone in, had I not seen the Drake preparing to come out...

Alarm smokes now appeared in great abundance, extending along on both sides of the channel. The tide was unfavourable, so that the Drake worked out but slowly. This obliged me to run down several times, and to lay with courses up, and maintopsail to the mast. At length the Drake weathered the point, and having led her out to about mid-channel, I suffered her to come within hail. The Drake hoisted English colours, and at the same instant, the American stars were displayed on board the Ranger. I expected that preface had been now at an end, but the enemy soon after hailed, demanding what ship it was? I directed the master to answer, "the American Continental ship Ranger; that we waited for them, and desired that they would come on; the sun was now little more than an hour from setting, it was therefore time to begin." The Drake being astern of the Ranger, I ordered the helm up, and gave her the first broadside. The action was warm, close, and obstinate. It lasted an hour and four minutes, when the enemy called for quarters; her fore and main-topsail yards being both cut away, and down on the cap; the top-gallant yard and mizen-gaff both hanging up and down along the mast; the second ensign which they had hoisted shot away, and hanging on the quarter gallery in the water; the jib shot away, and hanging in the water; her sails and rigging entirely cut to pieces; her masts and yards all wounded, and her hull also very much galled. I lost only Lieutenant Wallingsford and one seaman, John Dougall, killed, and six wounded; among whom are the gunner, Mr. Falls, and Mr. Powers, a midshipman, who lost his arm. One of the wounded, Nathaniel Wills, is since dead: the rest will recover. The loss of the enemy in killed and wounded, was far greater. All the prisoners allow, that they came out with a number not less than a hundred and sixty men: and many of them affirm that they amounted to a hundred and ninety. The medium may, perhaps, be the most exact account; and by that it will appear that they lost in killed and wounded, forty-two men. The captain and lieutenant were among the wounded; the former, having received a musket ball in the head the minute before they called for quarters, lived, and was sensible some time after my people boarded the prize. The lieutenant survived two days. They were buried with the honours due to their rank, and with the respect due to their memory.[47]

"Combat memorable entre le Pearson et Paul Jones"[48]

The Battle of Flamborough Head is also described in detail by Jones himself:

On the morning of that day, the 23d, the brig from Holland not being in sight, we chased a brigantine that appeared laying to, to windward. About noon, we saw and chased a large ship that appeared coming round Flamborough Head, from the northward, and at the same time I manned and armed one of the pilot boats to send in pursuit of the brigantine, which now appeared to be the vessel that I had forced ashore. Soon after this, a fleet of forty-one sail appeared off Flamborough Head, bearing N. N. E. This induced me to abandon the single ship which had then anchored in Burlington Bay; I also called back the pilot boat, and hoisted a signal for a general chase. When the fleet discovered us bearing down, all the merchant ships crowded sail towards the shore. The two ships of war that protected the fleet at the same time steered from the land, and made the disposition for battle.

[47] *Life and Correspondence of John Paul Jones*, by John Paul Jones, Janette Taylor (A. Chandler, 1830)
[48] Library of Congress http://www.loc.gov/pictures/item/89712610/

In approaching the enemy, I crowded every possible sail, and made the signal for the line of battle, to which the Alliance showed no attention. Earnest as I was for the action, I could not reach the commodore's ship until seven in the evening, being then within pistol shot, when he hailed the Bon Homme Richard. We answered him by firing a whole broadside.

The battle being thus begun, was continued with unremitting fury. Every method was practised on both sides to gain an advantage, and rake each other; and I must confess that the enemy's ship, being much more manageable than the Bon Homme Richard, gained thereby several times an advantageous situation, in spite of my best endeavours to prevent it. As I had to deal with an enemy of greatly superior force, I was under the necessity of closing with him, to prevent the advantage which he had over me in point of manoeuvre. It was my intention to lay the Bon Homme Richard athwart the enemy's bow; but as that operation required great dexterity in the management of both sails and helm, and some of our braces being shot away, it did not exactly succeed to my wish. The enemy's bowsprit, however, came over the Bon Homme Richard's poop by the mizen-mast, and I made both ships fast together in that situation, which, by the action of the wind on the enemy's sails, forced her stern close to the Bon Homme Richard's bow, so that the ships lay square alongside of each other, the yards being all entangled, and the cannon of each ship touching the opponent's. When this position took place, it was eight o'clock, previous to which the Bon Homme Richard had received sundry eighteen-pound shots below the water, and leaked very much. My battery of twelve-pounders, on which I had placed my chief dependence, being commanded by Lieutenant Dale and Colonel Weibert, and manned principally with American seamen and French volunteers, was entirely silenced and abandoned. As to the six old eighteen-pounders that formed the battery of the lower gun-deck, they did no service whatever, except firing eight shot in all. Two out of three of them burst at the first fire, and killed almost all the men who were stationed to manage them. Before this time, too, Colonel de Chamillard, who commanded a party of twenty soldiers on the poop, had abandoned that station after having lost some of his men. I had now only two pieces of cannon, (nine-pounders,) on the quarter-deck, that were not silenced, and not one of the heavier cannon was fired during the rest of the action. The purser, M. Mease, who commanded the guns on the quarterdeck, being dangerously wounded in the head, I was obliged to fill his place, and with great difficulty rallied a few men, and shifted over one of the lee quarter-deck guns, so that we afterwards played three pieces of nine-pounders upon the enemy. The tops alone seconded the fire of this little battery, and held out bravely during the whole of the action, especially the maintop, where Lieutenant Stack commanded. I directed the fire of one of the three cannon against the main-mast, with doubleheaded shot, while the other two were exceedingly well served with grape and canister shot, to silence the enemy's musketry and clear her decks, which was at last effected. The enemy were, as I have since understood, on the instant of calling for quarter, when the cowardice or treachery of three of my underofficers induced them to call to the enemy. The English commodore asked me if I demanded quarter, and I having answered him in the most determined negative, they renewed the battle with double fury. They were unable to stand the deck; but the fire of their cannon, especially the lower battery, which was entirely formed of ten-pounders, was incessant; both ships were set on fire in various places, and the scene was dreadful beyond the reach of language. To account for the timidity of my three under-officers, I mean, the gunner, the carpenter, and the master-at-arms, I must observe, that the two first were slightly wounded, and, as the ship had received various shot under water, and one of the pumps being shot away, the carpenter expressed his fears that she would sink, and the other two concluded that she was sinking, which occasioned the gunner to run aft on the poop, without my knowledge, to strike the colours. Fortunately for me, a cannon ball had done that before, by carrying away the ensign-staff; he was therefore reduced to the necessity of sinking, as he supposed, or of calling for quarter, and he preferred the latter.

All this time the Bon Homme Richard had sustained the action alone, and the enemy, though much superior in force, would have been very glad to have got clear, as appears by their own acknowledgments, and by their having let go an anchor the instant that I laid them on board, by which means they would have escaped, had I not made them well fast to the Bon Homme Richard.

At last, at half past nine o'clock, the Alliance appeared, and I now thought the battle at an end; but, to my utter astonishment, he discharged a broadside full into the stern of the Bon Homme

Richard. We called to him for God's sake to forbear firing into the Bon Homme Richard; yet they passed along the off side of the ship, and continued firing. There was no possibility of his mistaking the enemy's ship for the Bon Homme Richard, there being the most essential difference in their appearance and construction. Besides, it was then full moon light, and the sides of the Bon Homme Richard were all black, while the sides of the prize were all yellow. Yet, for the greater security, I showed the signal of our reconnoissance, by putting out three lanterns, one at the head, another at the stern, and the third in the middle, in a horizontal line. Every tongue cried that he was firing into the wrong ship, but nothing availed; he passed round, firing into the Bon Homme Richard's head, stern, and broadside, and by one of his volleys killed several of my best men, and mortally wounded a good officer on the forecastle only. My situation was really deplorable; the Bon Homme Richard received various shot under water from the Alliance; the leak gained on the pumps, and the fire increased much on board both ships. Some officers persuaded me to strike, of whose courage and good sense I entertain a high opinion. My treacherous master-at-arms let loose all my prisoners without my knowledge, and my prospects became gloomy indeed. I would not, however, give up the point. The enemy's main-mast began to shake, their firing decreased fast, ours rather increased, and the British colours were struck at half an hour past ten o'clock.[49]

The sharp-eyed reader will note that there is no mention of 'I have not yet begun to fight.' in the preceding account. This detail would be provided by Lieutenant Richard Dale, who described the opening verbal exchanges between the *HMS Serapis* and the *Bonhomme Richard*.

At about eight, being within hail, the Serapis demanded, 'What ship is that?' He was answered, 'I can't hear what you say.' Immediately after the Serapis hailed again, 'What ship is that? Answer immediately, or I shall be under the necessity of firing into you.' At this moment I received orders from Commodore Jones to commence the action with a broadside, which, indeed, appeared to be simultaneous on board both ships. Our position being to

---

[49] *Life and Correspondence of John Paul Jones*, by John Paul Jones, Janette Taylor (A. Chandler, 1830)

windward of the Serapis, we passed ahead of her, and the Serapis coming upon our larboard quarter, the action commenced abreast of each other. The Serapis soon passed ahead of the Bon Homme Richard, and when he thought he had gained a distance sufficient to go down athwart the forefoot to rake us, found he had not enough distance, and that the Bon Homme Richard would be aboard him, put his helm alee, which brought the two ships on a line; and the Bon Homme Richard having headway, ran her bows into the stern of the Serapis. We had remained in this situation but a few minutes, when we were again hailed by the Serapis; 'Has your ship struck?' To which Captain Jones answered, 'I have not yet begun to fight.' [50]

The *Bonhomme Richard* didn't survive the attack, but Jones and most of the crew transferred to the *HMS Serapis*.

While Jones won several awards for his bravery and service from the King of France and the Continental Congress, the latter couldn't seem to find a job for him to do after he returned to America. In the final years of his life, he worked as a mercenary for Empress Catherine II of Russia as a rear admiral - he would be pressed into naval operations against the Turks.

John Paul Jones died on July 18, 1792 in Paris, France.

---

[50] *Life and Correspondence of John Paul Jones*, by John Paul Jones, Janette Taylor (A. Chandler, 1830)

Marquis de Lafayette

Date	Events
September 6, 1757	Born in Chavaniac, Auvergne, France
August 1, 1759	Lafayette's father dies after being struck by a cannon ball at the Battle of Minden in Westphalia
1771	Completes studies at Collège du Plessis, and trains in the *Musketeers of military Household of King of France*
December 7, 1776	Arranges to become a Major General in the Continental Army
1777	The French government grants one million livres in supplies to the Continental Army
June 13, 1777	Arrives by ship in South Carolina, after being pursued by the British
July 31, 1777	Continental Congress commissions Lafayette as a Major General, but assigns him no troops
August 10, 1777	At the urging of Benjamin Franklin, General George Washington meets with Lafayette in Bucks County, Pennsylvania. Lafayette joins Washington's staff.
September 11, 1777+	Wounded in the leg at the Battle of Brandywine, and helps ensure an ordered retreat. Lafayette recuperates with the Moravians in Bethlehem. Washington recommends to Congress that Lafayette be given a division command.
November 24, 1777	Defeats a Hessian force at the Battle of Gloucester, New Jersey
Winter 1777/78	• Winter at Valley Forge • Warns Washington of the *Conway Cabal*, which hoped to replace Washington with Horatio Gates • After being shipped to Albany, New York by the War Board as part of the Conway Plot, Lafayette recruits the Oneida tribe to the American cause
February 6, 1778	Treaty between France and the United States signed
May 20, 1778	Slips away from a vastly larger British force at the

Date	Events
	Battle of Barren Hill (now Lafayette Hill, Pennsylvania)
June 28, 1778	Helps Washington drive the British from the field in the Battle of Monmouth, after General Charles Lee almost leads the Continental Army to defeat
July 8, 1778	French fleet arrives in Rhode Island under Admiral d'Estaing
August 29, 1778	Battle of Rhode Island (Aquidneck Island, Rhode Island). After a poorly coordinated joint action between the Americans and the French at Newport, the British keep control of Aquidneck Island
February 1779	• Lafayette returns to Paris, and is promptly imprisoned by King Louis XVI for 8 days for leaving France without the king's permission • Louis XVI meets with Lafayette, and reestablishes his military position in France • Lafayette is presented with a sword commissioned by the Continental Congress • Lafayette and Benjamin Franklin secure 6,000 troops under General Jean-Baptiste de Rochambeau, to fight with the Continental Army
April 28, 1779	Returns to America after having secured an additional 5,500 French troops
August 1780	In command of two light infantry brigades north of New York City
February 1781	In command of three regiments, Lafayette is sent to Virginia to replace von Steuben
July 6, 1781	Battle of Green Spring (James City County, Virginia), in which Lafayette and Mad Anthony Wayne escape a trap laid by Cornwallis
August 1781	Lafayette begins the entrapment of Yorktown by positioning his troops on Malvern Hill
September 14, 1781	Washington's Army arrives, and joins Lafayette
September 28, 1781	Washington begins attacks on Yorktown
October 14, 1781	Lafayette's forces seize Redoubt 9; Alexander Hamilton takes Redoubt 10
October 19,	Cornwallis surrenders

Date	Events
1781	
1787	*Edict of Versailles* passed in France granting tolerance to Protestants (mostly Huguenots), at the urging of Lafayette
July 1791	Orders the *Garde nationale* to fire on protesters in Champ de Mars
August 1792	Tries to escape from French Revolutionaries, but is captured by the Austrians, who imprison him for 5 years
1797	Released from prison after the intercession of Napoleon Bonaparte
1824/25	Triumphant tour of all 24 states in the United States
May 20, 1834	Dies in Paris, France. He is buried in soil from Bunker Hill.
June 24, 1905	Granted honorary United States citizenship

The Marquis de Lafayette was born in Auvergne in south central France in 1757. Attracted to the American cause, Lafayette joined the American war effort on December 7, 1776, when he was appointed as a major-general in the Continental Army. He was wounded at the Battle of Brandywine, and after a brief recuperation period, he wintered at Valley Forge.

Lafayette quickly became one of Washington's most trusted subordinates and was, at various times, commander of multiple brigades and regiments. He warned Washington of the *Conway Cabal*, which hoped to replace Washington with Horatio Gates. Lafayette was briefly exiled by Washington's enemies in Rhode Island for his efforts.

While an adequate commander in the field (Gloucester, Monmouth, Barren Hill, Yorktown), Lafayette's greatest contribution to the patriot's war effort came with his unceasing work in establishing a closer tie between France and the Continentals. On February 6, 1778, a treaty between

France and the United States was signed. Lafayette took part in the celebration by Washington's army at Valley Forge. In 1779, Lafayette procured over 10,000 troops from French king Louis XVI.

Washington and Lafayette at Valley Forge[51]

Lafayette's contribution to the patriot cause has never been forgotten. In 1824, Lafayette made a triumphant tour of all 24 states in the United States. In World War I, when General John Pershing arrived in France, he is said to have remarked "Lafayette, we are here". American fighter pilots in World War I fought in the *Lafayette Escadrille*.

[51] Library of Congress http://www.loc.gov/pictures/item/91792202/

James Madison

Date	Event
March 16, 1751	Born in Port Conway, Virginia
1764	House at Montpelier built
1769	Co-founds the American Whig Society (a student debating organization) at Princeton
1771	Graduates from the College of New Jersey (Princeton University)
March 1, 1781 – November 1, 1783	Delegate to the Congress of the Confederation (Virginia)
May 25, 1787 - September 17, 1787	Delegate to the Constitutional Convention in Philadelphia
May 29, 1787	Madison writes the *Virginia Plan*, which becomes the basis for debate during the Constitutional Convention
1788	The Federalist Papers, written by Alexander Hamilton, John Jay and James Monroe published
1798/99	Drafts (with Thomas Jefferson) the *Kentucky and Virginia Resolutions*, which opposed the *Alien and Sedition Act* of John Adams. Madison and Jefferson champion states rights over Federal rights.
March 4, 1789 – March 4, 1793	Member of the U.S. House of Representatives (Virginia, 5th district)
June 8, 1789	James Madison introduces a series of amendments to the Constitution that contains what will later be called the *Bill of Rights*
September 25, 1789	Congress approves what will later be known as the *Bill of Rights*, and sends the amendments to the states for ratification
December 15, 1791	Amendments 1-10, or the *Bill of Rights* are ratified by the states, and become part of the U.S. Constitution
1791	With Thomas Jefferson, forms the Democratic-Republican Party

Date	Event
March 4, 1793 – March 4, 1797	Member of the U.S. House of Representatives (Virginia, 15th district)
September 15, 1794	Marries Dolley (or Dolly) Payne Todd
1801	Madison inherits Montpelier and his father's 108 slaves upon the death of his father
May 2, 1801 – March 3, 1809	United States Secretary of State (under Thomas Jefferson)
1803/04	Oversees Louisiana Purchase
February 24, 1803	*Marbury v. Madison* decided by the Supreme Court. It settled that the Supreme Court had the right to decide whether laws passed by Congress met Constitutional muster.
July 4, 1803	Louisiana Purchase from Napoleon, for $15,000,000
1805	• Madison Range (Montana and Idaho) so-named by Lewis and Clark • Madison River (Montana) so-named by Lewis and Clark
March 4, 1809 March 4, 1817	President of the United States
November 7, 1811	General William Henry Harrison defeats *Tecumseh's Confederacy* at the Battle of Tippecanoe (near Lafayette, Indiana)
April 30, 1812	Louisiana joins the United States
November 26, 1812	Sloop *USS Madison* launched for service on the Great lakes
June 18, 1812 – February 18, 1815	War of 1812
September 10, 1813	British defeated at the Battle of Lake Erie
October 5, 1813	General William Henry Harrison defeats the British and their Indian allies at the Battle of the Thames (Ontario). Indian chief Tecumseh is killed.
August 24, 1814	• British victory at the Battle of Bladensburg (Maryland) • British attack on Washington; Dolly (or Dolley) Madison saves silver and documents from the White House. A painting of George Washington

Date	Event
	is also saved. The White House and Capitol are burned.
September 12/15, 1814	Americans defeat the British at Baltimore. Francis Scott Key is inspired to write the *Star Spangled Banner* after watching the bombardment of Fort McHenry.
December 24, 1814	Treaty of Ghent (Belgium) signed (but not ratified), ending the War of 1812
December 30, 1814	Treaty of Ghent ratified by Parliament
January 8, 1815	Stunning victory by Andrew Jackson over the British in New Orleans
February 18, 1815	Treaty of Ghent approved by the U.S. Senate
March 3, 1815	Use of naval force in the Second Barbary War authorized by Congress
December 11, 1816	Indiana joins the United States
1816/25	*Era of Good Feelings*, as the young nation gains confidence after the victory over the British in the War of 1812
1817	Retires to his plantation Montpelier, in Orange County, Virginia
1826	President of the University of Virginia
1829	Appointed as a representative to the constitutional convention in Richmond for the revising of the Virginia state constitution
1832	Van Buren-class schooner *USS Madison* is a built for the United States Revenue Service
June 28, 1836	Dies in Orange County, Virginia. He is buried at Montpelier.
1848	Madison, Wisconsin incorporated
1865	Former slave Paul Jennings writes *A Colored Man's Reminiscences of James Madison*
December 10, 1894	$2 stamp honoring James Madison issued by the United States Post office
June 5, 1903	$2 stamp honoring James Madison issued by the United States Post office
1908	James Madison University in Harrisonburg, Virginia established

Date	Event
1928/34	Madison appears on the U.S. $5,000.00 bill
July 1, 1938	4¢ stamp issued by the United States Post office
October 20, 1939	Benson-class destroyer *USS Madison* (DD-425) launched
December 19, 1960	Montpelier designated a National Historic Landmark
March 15, 1963	*USS James Madison* (SSBN-627) ballistic submarine launched
October 15, 1966	Montpelier added to the National Register of Historic Places
1986	Congress established the James Madison Memorial Fellowship Foundation, focused on assisting educators in grades 7-12 in teaching civics and the U.S. Constitution
May 22, 1986	22¢ stamp issued by the United States Postal Service
October 18, 2001	34¢ commemorative stamp (250th anniversary of his birth) issued by the United States Postal Service

Unlike some of our heroes and heroines, who played important roles before and during the American Revolution, James Madison's influence would occur mostly after the the Revolution was over. Perhaps most importantly, Madison is sometimes referred to as the "Father of the Constitution".

Madison served as a delegate to the Constitutional Convention in Philadelphia between May 25, 1787 - September 17, 1787. On May 29, 1787, Madison wrote the *Virginia Plan*, which became the basis for debate during the Constitutional Convention. Madison was also a key player in the ratification of the Constitution in two major states – Virginia and New York. In Virginia, he out-orated Patrick Henry (who was against the ratification), and in New York, Madison joined with Alexander Hamilton and John Jay to write the *Federalist Papers*, which interpreted the fledgling Constitution in detail. Even today, the *Federalist Papers* are a key document (or set of documents) in interpreting the original intentions of the Founding Fathers in interpreting the Constitution.

"James Madison, 4th president of the United States"[52]

Madison wasn't done with the Constitution, though, even after it was ratified. He had been concerned that there wasn't a statement of individual rights in the Constitution protecting the individual from the state. On June 8, 1789, he introduced a series of amendments to the Constitution that contained what will later be called the *Bill of Rights*. On December 15, 1791, Amendments 1-10, or the *Bill of Rights* were ratified by the states, and became part of the U.S. Constitution.

The finalized Bill of Rights appears below:

Amendment I

---

[52] Library of Congress http://www.loc.gov/pictures/item/2003679975/

Congress shall make no law respecting an establishment of religion, or prohibiting the free exercise thereof; or abridging the freedom of speech, or of the press; or the right of the people peaceably to assemble, and to petition the Government for a redress of grievances.

Amendment II
A well regulated Militia, being necessary to the security of a free State, the right of the people to keep and bear Arms, shall not be infringed.

Amendment III
No Soldier shall, in time of peace be quartered in any house, without the consent of the Owner, nor in time of war, but in a manner to be prescribed by law.

Amendment IV
The right of the people to be secure in their persons, houses, papers, and effects, against unreasonable searches and seizures, shall not be violated, and no Warrants shall issue, but upon probable cause, supported by Oath or affirmation, and particularly describing the place to be searched, and the persons or things to be seized.

Amendment V
No person shall be held to answer for a capital, or otherwise infamous crime, unless on a presentment or indictment of a Grand Jury, except in cases arising in the land or naval forces, or in the Militia, when in actual service in time of War or public danger; nor shall any person be subject for the same offence to be twice put in jeopardy of life or limb; nor shall be compelled in any criminal case to be a witness against himself, nor be deprived of life, liberty, or property, without due process of law; nor shall private property be taken for public use, without just compensation.

Amendment VI
In all criminal prosecutions, the accused shall enjoy the right to a speedy and public trial, by an impartial jury of the State and district wherein the crime shall have been committed, which district shall have been previously ascertained by law, and to be informed of the nature and cause of the accusation; to be confronted with the witnesses against him; to have compulsory

process for obtaining witnesses in his favor, and to have the Assistance of Counsel for his defence.

Amendment VII
In Suits at common law, where the value in controversy shall exceed twenty dollars, the right of trial by jury shall be preserved, and no fact tried by a jury, shall be otherwise re-examined in any Court of the United States, than according to the rules of the common law.

Amendment VIII
Excessive bail shall not be required, nor excessive fines imposed, nor cruel and unusual punishments inflicted.

Amendment IX
The enumeration in the Constitution, of certain rights, shall not be construed to deny or disparage others retained by the people.

Amendment X
The powers not delegated to the United States by the Constitution, nor prohibited by it to the States, are reserved to the States respectively, or to the people.

In a letter to Thomas Jefferson dated October 17, 1788, Madison discusses why a bill of rights is necessary in a democracy:

What use, then, it may be asked, can a bill of rights serve in popular Governments? I answer, the two following, which, though less essential than in other Governments [monarchies], sufficiently recommend the precaution: 1. The political truths declared in that solemn manner acquire by degrees the character of fundamental maxims of free Government, and as they become incorporated with the National sentiment, counteract the impulses of interest and passion. 2. Although it be generally true, as above stated, that the danger of oppression lies in the interested majorities of the people rather than in usurped acts of the Government, yet there may be occasions on which the evil may spring from the latter source; and on such, a bill of rights will be a good ground for an appeal to the sense of the community. Perhaps, too, there may be a certain degree of danger that a succession of artful and ambitious rulers may, by gradual and well-timed advances, finally erect an independent Government on the subversion of liberty. Should this danger exist at all, it is prudent to guard against it, especially when the precaution can do no injury.[53]

Madison served as United States Secretary of State (under Thomas Jefferson) from May 2, 1801 – March 3, 1809, and as such, he was intimately involved in the negotiations for the Louisiana Purchase. It was Madison who provided the Constitutional justification for the purchase.

Madison served in various posts as a politician, including:

- Delegate to the Congress of the Confederation (Virginia) (March 1, 1781 – November 1, 1783)
- Delegate to the Constitutional Convention in Philadelphia (May 25, 1787 - September 17, 1787)
- Member of the U.S. House of Representatives (Virginia, 5th district) (March 4, 1789 – March 4, 1793)
- Member of the U.S. House of Representatives (Virginia, 15th district) (March 4, 1793 – March 4, 1797)
- President of the United States (March 4, 1809 March 4, 1817)
- Representative to the constitutional convention in Richmond for the revising of the Virginia state constitution (1829)

As president, Madison oversaw the victory of the United States against Great Britain in the War of 1812, but suffered the indignity of having his home (the White House) burned by the British. A former slave of James Madison, Paul Jennings, describes the scene at the White House when the British were getting close on August 24, 1814:

---

[53] *Letters and Other Writings of James Madison: 1769-1793*, by James Madison (J.B. Lippincott & Co., 1865)

Well, on the 24th of August, sure enough, the British reached Bladensburg [Maryland], and the fight began between 11 and 12. Even that very morning General Armstrong assured Mrs. Madison there was no danger. The President, with General Armstrong, General Winder, Colonel Monroe, Richard Rush, Mr. Graham, Tench Ringgold, and Mr. Duvall, rode out on horseback to Bladensburg to see how things looked. Mrs. Madison ordered dinner to be ready at 3, as usual; I set the table myself, and

brought up the ale, cider, and wine, and placed them in the coolers, as all the Cabinet and several military gentlemen and strangers were expected. While waiting, at just about 3, as Sukey, the house-servant, was lolling out of a chamber window, James Smith, a free colored man who had accompanied Mr. Madison to Bladensburg, galloped up to the house, waving his hat, and cried out, "Clear out, clear out! General Armstrong has ordered a retreat!" All then was confusion. Mrs. Madison ordered her carriage, and passing through the dining-room, caught up what silver she could crowd into her old-fashioned reticule [a small purse or bag], and then jumped into the chariot with her servant girl Sukey, and Daniel Carroll, who took charge of them; Jo. Bolin drove them over to Georgetown Heights; the British were expected in a few minutes. Mr. Cutts, her brother-in-law, sent me to a stable on 14th street, for his carriage. People were running in every direction. John Freeman (the colored butler) drove off in the coachee with his wife, child, and servant; also a feather bed lashed on behind the coachee, which was all the furniture saved, except part of the silver and the portrait of Washington...

I will here mention that although the British were expected every minute, they did not arrive for some hours; in the mean time, a rabble, taking advantage of the confusion, ran all over the White House, and stole lots of silver and whatever they could lay their hands on.[54]

---

[54] *A Colored Man's Reminiscences of James Madison*, by Paul Jennings (George C. Beadle, 1865) Dolly Madison miniature: Yale University Art Gallery. Public domain.

Washington, D.C., August 24, 1814. "Print shows British soldiers in the foreground and British ships on the Potomac River bombarding Washington, D.C., which appears atop a hill, with several buildings burning.", 1815 engraving[55]

Madison also oversaw as President the authorization of naval forces in the Second Barbary War, and the entry of Indiana and Louisiana as states into the Union. The period between 1816/25 is often referred to as the *Era of Good Feelings*, as the young nation gained confidence after the victory over the British in the War of 1812. The *Era of Good Feelings* is almost entirely attributed to James Madison.

It should be noted that James Madison, along with Thomas Jefferson, formed the Democratic-Republican Party in 1791, as a counter-balance to Federalists such as Alexander Hamilton and John Adams.

In addition to the many town names, ships, and postage stamp issues that honor Madison, the following states have counties named after him: Alabama, Arkansas, Florida, Georgia, Idaho, Illinois, Indiana, Iowa, Kentucky, Louisiana, Mississippi, Missouri, Montana, Nebraska, New York, North Carolina, Ohio, Tennessee, Texas and Virginia.

---

[55] Library of Congress http://www.loc.gov/pictures/item/2012645366/

Francis Marion

The Washington of the south, he steadily pursued the warfare most safe for us, and most fatal to our enemies. He taught us to sleep in the swamps, to feed on roots, to drink the turbid waters of the ditch, to prowl nightly round the encampments of the foe, like lions round the habitations of the shepherds what had slaughtered their cubs. Sometimes he taught us to fall upon the enemy by surprise, distracting the midnight hour with the horrors of our battle: at other times, when our forces were increased, he led us on boldly to the charge, hewing the enemy to pieces, under the approving light of day. Oh, Marion, my friend! my friend! never can I forget thee. Although thy wars are all ended, and thyself at rest in the grave, yet I see thee still. I see thee as thou wert wont to ride, most terrible in battle to the enemies of thy country. Thine eyes like balls of fire, flamed beneath thy lowering brows. But lovely still wert thou in mercy, thou bravest among the sons of men! For, soon as the enemy sinking under our swords, cried for quarter, thy heart swelled with commiseration, and thy countenance was changed, even as the countenance of a man who beheld the slaughter of his brothers. The basest Tory who could but touch the hem of thy garment was safe. The avengers of blood stopped short in thy presence, and turned away abashed from the lightning of thine eyes.[56] (Peter Horry)

Date	Events
c.1732	Born in Berkeley County, South Carolina
c. 1747/48	Francis is shipwrecked on his way to the West Indies
January 1, 1757	Francis and his brother are recruited by the British to fight Cherokees in the French and Indian War
1761	Promoted to lieutenant, and serves under Captain William Moultrie against the Cherokee
June 7, 1761	Battle of Etchoee against the Cherokees. Marion led the initial assault in the 6 hour battle, which was a defeat for the Indians
June 21, 1775	Receives a commission as Captain in the 2nd South Carolina Regiment. Once again, he will serve under William Moultrie.

---

[56] *The Life of General Francis Marion*, by Mason Locke Weems, Peter Horry (J. B. Lippincott, 1860)

Date	Events
1776/79	Involved in building, defending and commanding Fort Sullivan (now Fort Moultrie) in Charleston harbor
June 1776	Defends Fort Sullivan in Charleston Harbor
September 1776	Commissioned as a Lieutenant Colonel by the Continental Congress
1779	Participates in the siege of Savannah (which fails)
May 12, 1780	Charleston falls to Henry Clinton, but Marion had left the city with a broken ankle several days before
August 1780	Assigned by Horatio Gates to take command of the Williamsburg Militia in the Pee Dee River area, and act as a scout. Marion begins his hit and run tactics against the British for which he will become famous.
September 14, 1780	Battle of Black Mingo near Willtown, South Carolina. Marion scatters a group of Tory loyalists into the nearby swamps. Marion's recruitment efforts go up after this battle.
November 1780	Colonel Banastre Tarleton is sent by Cornwallis to find Francis Marion. Tarleton fails, and refers to Marion as that "damn old fox". Marion is appointed brigadier general of state troops by by South Carolina governor Gov. John Rutledge.
December 1780	Marion begins using Snow's Island as his base of operations
January 1781	Marion and Henry "Light Horse Harry" Lee launch an unsuccessful attack on Georgetown, SC
March 1781	Marion's Snow's Island camp is destroyed by British Colonel Welbone Doyle
April 23, 1781	Marion and Lee capture Fort Watson (near Summerton, South Carolina) after a week long siege
May 1781	Marion and Lee capture Fort Motte (South Carolina) after a five day siege
August 31, 1781	Marion rescues American soldiers trapped by a British force of 500
September 8, 1781	Commands 240 men of Greene's army at Battle of Eutaw Springs
January 1782	Elected to a new State Assembly at Jacksonborough
June 1782	Defeats a Loyalist force near the Pee Dee River
December 1782	British withdrawal from Charleston, SC

Date	Events
1784	Marion is named commander of Fort Johnson, South Carolina, and receives an annual stipend
1786	Marries his cousin Mary Esther Videau
1790	One of the authors of the constitution of South Carolina
February 27, 1795	Dies at his estate, Pond Bluff, and is buried at the Belle Isle Plantation Cemetery, Berkeley County, South Carolina
c. 1800	Marion County, South Carolina is so-named
1805	*The Life of General Francis Marion* by Parson Weems and Brigadier General Peter Horry is published, turning the Swamp Fox into an international superstar
1839	Marion, Iowa incorporated
July 10, 1936	Francis Marion National Forest, north of Charleston, is established
1959/61	Walt Disney releases the eight-part series *The Swamp Fox,* starring Leslie Nielsen as Francis Marion, turning the Swamp Fox into an international superstar
1970	Francis Marion University established near Florence, South Carolina
December 2, 1974	Snow's Island is designated a National Historic Landmark
2000	The Benjamin Martin (Mel Gibson) character in *The Patriot* is based on Francis Marion

Prior to August 1780, Marion had had a distinguished but not especially notable military career. He had served in the French and Indian War, primarily against the Cherokee. He had been involved in the building, defending and commanding of Fort Sullivan (now Fort Moultrie) in Charleston Harbor.

But in August 1780, everything would change. Horatio Gates (quite unimpressed by Marion and his men) assigned Marion to take command of the Williamsburg Militia in the Pee Dee (or PeeDee) River area, and act as a scout. It was at this point that Marion began his hit and run tactics against the British for which he would become famous. In a series of surprise attacks, Marion had a devastating effect on the British efforts in the South Carolina countryside.

"Marion's brigade crossing the Pedee River, S.C.. 1778. On their way to attack the British force under Tarleton"[57]

In November 1780, Colonel Banastre Tarleton was sent by Lord Cornwallis to destroy Francis Marion's force. Marion led him on an jaunt through 26 miles of swamp. Tarleton never caught up with him, and was quoted as saying "As for this damned old fox, the Devil himself could not catch him." Soon, the local people that Marion championed were referring to him as the "Swamp Fox". Because of his success against the British, Marion was promoted to brigadier general of state troops by South Carolina governor Gov. John Rutledge.

Marion was one of the greatest guerrilla fighters in American history, a technique he probably learned from the Cherokees in the French and Indian War. He was especially skilled at turning irregulars and local militia into skilled marauders. And

---

[57] Library of Congress http://www.loc.gov/pictures/item/2006691581/

like Nathan Bedford Forest in the Civil War, Marion had no formal military training (although he did have military experience).

From December 1780 to March 1781, Marion used Snow's Island as his base of operations. It was a natural defensive position, accessible only by water (after the bridges were destroyed). It was used as the base for both his hit and run activities, and his unsuccessful attack on Georgetown with Henry "Light Horse Harry" Lee. In Walt Disney's *Swamp Fox*, much of the action takes place on the island. Marion's Snow's Island camp was destroyed by British Colonel Welbone Doyle in March 1781.

Below are three extracts from early sources regarding Snow's Island. The first, from Parson Weems, talks about Snow's Island in general terms.

> ...he always kept a snug hiding place in reserve for us; which was Snow's Island, a most romantic spot, and admirably fitted to our use. Nature had guarded it, nearly all around, with deep waters and inaccessible marshes; and the neighboring gentlemen were all rich, and hearty whigs, who acted by us the double part of generous stewards and faithful spies, so that, while there, we lived at once in safety and plenty.[58]

The second extract tells about the hardships endured by Marion and his (generally unpaid) men.

> His men were badly clothed in homespun, a light wear which afforded little warmth. They slept in the open air, and frequently without a blanket. Their ordinary food consisted of sweet potatoes, garnished, on fortunate occasions, with lean beef. Salt was only to be had when they succeeded in the capture of an enemy's commissariat; and even when this most necessary of all human condiments was obtained, the unselfish nature of Marion

---

[58] *The Life of General Francis Marion*, by Mason Locke Weems, Peter Horry (J. B. Lippincott, 1860)

made him indifferent to its use. He distributed it on such occasions, in quantities not exceeding a bushel, to each Whig family; and by this patriarchal care, still farther endeared himself to the affection of his followers.[59]

Finally, we present the oft-told story of a young British officer dispatched to Snow's Island to facilitate a prisoner exchange with Marion. In it, we get a description of the camp, of Marion's men, and the impact Marion could have on people.

It appears that, desiring the exchange of prisoners, a young officer was dispatched from the British post at Georgetown to the swamp encampment of Marion, in order to effect this object. He was encountered by one of the scouting parties of the brigade, carefully blindfolded, and conducted, by intricate paths, through the wild passes, and into the deep recesses of the island. Here, when his eyes were uncovered, he found himself surrounded by a motley multitude, which might well have reminded him of Robin Hood and his outlaws. The scene was unquestionably wonderfully picturesque and attractive, and our young officer seems to have been duly impressed by it. He was in the middle of one of those grand natural amphitheaters so common in our swamp forests, in which the massive pine, the gigantic cypress, and the stately and ever-green laurel, streaming with moss, and linking their opposite arms, inflexibly locked in the embrace of centuries, group together, with elaborate limbs and leaves, the chief and most graceful features of Gothic architecture. To these recesses, through the massed foliage of the forest, the sunlight came as sparingly, and with rays as mellow and subdued, as through the painted window of the old cathedral, falling upon aisle and chancel. Scattered around were the forms of those hardy warriors with whom our young officer was yet destined, most probably, to meet in conflict, —strange or savage in costume or attitude—lithe and sinewy of frame—keen-eyed and wakeful at the least alarm. Some slept, some joined in boyish sports; some with foot in stirrup, stood ready for the signal to mount and march. The deadly rifle leaned against the tree, the sabre depended from its boughs. Steeds were browsing in the shade, with loosened bits, but saddled, ready at the first sound of the bugle to skirr [move

---

[59] *The Life of Francis Marion*, by William Gilmore Simm (George F. Cooledge & Brother, 1813)

rapidly] through brake and thicket. Distant fires, dimly burning, sent up their faint white smokes, that, mingling with the thick forest tops, which they could not pierce, were scarce distinguishable from the long grey moss which made the old trees look like so many ancient patriarchs. But the most remarkable object in all this scene was Marion himself. Could it be that the person who stood before our visitor—" in stature of the smallest size, thin, as well as low—was that of the redoubted chief, whose sleepless activity and patriotic zeal had carried terror to the gates of Charleston; had baffled the pursuit and defied the arms of the best British captains; had beaten the equal enemy, and laughed at the superior? Certainly, if he were, then never were the simple resources of intellect, as distinguishable from strength of limb, or powers of muscle, so wonderfully evident as in this particular instance. The physical powers of Marion were those simply of endurance. His frame had an iron hardihood, derived from severe discipline and subdued desires and appetites, but lacked the necessary muscle and capacities of the mere soldier. It was as the general, the commander, the counsellor, rather than as the simple leader of his men, that Marion takes rank, and is to be considered in the annals of war. He attempted no physical achievements, and seems to have placed very little reliance upon his personal prowess...

The young officer, as soon as his business was dispatched, prepared to depart, but Marion gently detained him, as he said, for dinner, which was in preparation. "The mild and dignified simplicity of Marion's manners had already produced their effects, and, to prolong so interesting an interview, the invitation was accepted. The entertainment was served up on pieces of bark, and consisted entirely of roasted potatoes, of which the general ate heartily, requesting his guest to profit by his example, repeating the old adage, that 'hunger is the best sauce.' "But surely, general," said the officer, "this cannot be your ordinary fare." "Indeed, sir, it is," he replied, " and we are fortunate on this occasion, entertaining company, to have more than our usual allowance." The story goes, that the young Briton was so greatly impressed with the occurrence, that, on his return to Georgetown, he retired from the service, **declaring his conviction that men who could with such content endure the privations of such a life, were not to be subdued.** His conclusion was strictly logical, and hence, indeed, the importance of such a warfare as

127

that carried on by Marion, in which, if he obtained no great victories, he was yet never to be overcome.[60] (emphasis added)

"Gen. Marion in his swamp encampment inviting a British officer to dinner"[61]

In the last twenty years or so, there have been diligent efforts on the part of the politically correct to attempt to de-mythologize Marion, and turn him into a character of scorn. Their argument usually includes points such as these (my response in parenthesis):

- Marion was mean to the Indians! (Of course, this occurred during a WAR between England on one side, and the French and their Indian allies on the other. That's why its called the French and Indian War).

---

[60] *The Life of Francis Marion*, by William Gilmore Simm (George F. Cooledge & Brother, 1813)
[61] Library of Congress http://www.loc.gov/pictures/item/2003663990/

- Marion kept slaves! (I'm shocked, shocked to hear that an 18th century plantation owner in South Carolina would own slaves. He should be singled out for scorn!)
- Marion was mean to the British during the Revolutionary War (Of course, Marion was fighting against Banastre Tarleton, possibly the most vicious British officer in the Revolutionary War. Tarleton ordered the massacre of Colonial troops at the Battle of Waxhaws after they had raised a white flag.)
- The first major biography about Francis Marion was written by that Parson Weems guy. Isn't he the one that made up the cherry tree story about George Washington? Can't believe anything he says (Weems book is based on a manuscript written by Colonel Peter Horry who served under Marion)

Parson Weems describes an incident in his biography of Marion whereby a British officer lectures Marion on his style of guerrilla warfare. Marion's reply (second paragraph below) pretty much says it all:

The next morning [British] colonel Watson sent a flag over to Marion, whom he charged with carrying on war in a manner entirely different from all civilized nations. "Why sir," said he to Marion, "you must certainly command a horde of savages, who delight in nothing but murder. I can't cross a swamp or a bridge, but I am waylaid and shot at as if I were a mad dog. Even my sentries are fired at and killed on their posts. Why, my God, sir! this is not the way that Christians ought to fight!"

To this Marion replied, that "he was sorry to be obliged to say, that from what he had known of them, the British officers were the last men on earth who had any right to preach about honor and humanity. That for men to come three thousand miles to plunder and hang an innocent people, and then to tell that people how they ought to fight, betrayed an ignorance and impudence which he fain would hope had no parallel in the history of man.

That for his part, he always believed, and still did believe that he should be doing God and his country good service to surprise and kill such men, while they continued this diabolical warfare, as he would the wolves and panthers of the forest."[62]

The list of states that have towns or counties named after Francis Marion include Alabama, Arkansas, Connecticut, Florida, Georgia, Idaho, Illinois, Indiana, Iowa, Kentucky, Louisiana, Maine, Maryland, Massachusetts, Michigan, Minnesota, Mississippi, Missouri, Montana, Nebraska, New Jersey, New York, North Carolina, North Dakota, Ohio, Oregon, Pennsylvania, South Carolina, South Dakota, Tennessee, Texas, Virginia, West Virginia and Wisconsin.[63]

It was because of men like Francis Marion that we have the freedoms that we enjoy today in the United States of America.

---

[62] *The Life of General Francis Marion*, by Mason Locke Weems, Peter Horry (J. B. Lippincott, 1860)
[63] http://en.wikipedia.org/wiki/List_of_places_named_for_Francis_Marion

Daniel Morgan

Date	Events
July 6, 1736	Born in Hunterdon County, New Jersey
1755	Becomes a teamster in the French and Indian War, with his cousin Daniel Boone
1756	Punished with 499 lashes at Old Fort Chiswell because he hit a superior officer. He would carry the scars for the rest of his life.
1758	Wounded in an ambush by Indians
1763	Begins co-habitation with Abigail Curry[64]
1774	• Fights against the Shawnee (Dunmore's War) in the Ohio Country • Marries Abigail Bailey
June 1775	The Virginia House of Burgesses appoints Daniel Morgan captain, and puts him in charge of 1 of 2 rifle companies
August 6, 1775	Arrives in Boston, Massachusetts with rifle company *Morgan's Riflemen*
September 25, 1775	Departs for Canada with three companies under the command of Benedict Arnold
December 31, 1775	Colonial Army beaten at the Battle of Quebec; Morgan is captured
January 1777	Released in a prisoner exchange; promoted to Colonel for his exploits during the Battle of Quebec, and put in command of the 11th Virginia Regiment of the Continental Line
June 13, 1777	Provisional Rifle Corps, a light infantry unit, is added to Morgan's command; Morgan is assigned to harassing Howe's rear-guard across New Jersey
August 30, 1777	Assigned to the command of Horatio Gates
October 7, 1777	Colonial victory at Saratoga
September 14, 1778	Takes command of the 7th Virginia Regiment
June 30, 1779	Resigns from the Continental Army when he is not

---

[64] Some sources say Abigail Bailey. Also, some sources say this was the year they were married.

Date	Events
	promoted to Brigadier General
August 1780	Joins the Southern Command under Horatio Gates
October 13, 1780	Brigadier General Daniel Morgan
December 3, 1780	Meets with new Southern Command leader Nathanael Greene in Charlotte, North Carolina. Morgan is assigned to hit-and-run operations in South Carolina with about 700 men
January 17, 1781	Morgan defeats Banastre Tarleton at the Battle of Cowpens
July 1781	Morgan and LaFayette pursue Tarleton in Virginia, but do not catch him
1782	• After the war, Morgan joins the Presbyterian Church and builds a house near Winchester, Virginia • Daniel Morgan House ("Saratoga") near Winchester, Virginia is completed
1785	Burwell-Morgan Mill near Millwood, Clarke County, Virginia us built. The grist mill is still open today, and is on the National Register of Historic Places.
1790	Awarded a gold medal by the Congress for his victory at Cowpens
1794	Commands a wing of the army into Western Pennsylvania during the Whiskey Rebellion
March 4, 1797 – March 3, 1799	Congressman from Virginia
July 6, 1802	Dies in Winchester, Virginia
December 10, 1807	Morgan County, Georgia formed
December 29, 1817	Morgan County, Ohio formed
1817	Morgan County, Tennessee formed
1820	Morgan County (West) Virginia formed
June 14, 1821	Cotaco County Alabama renamed to Morgan County
December 7, 1822	Morgan County, Kentucky formed
1822	Morgan County, Indiana formed
1823	Morgan County, Illinois formed
January 5,	Morgan County, Missouri formed

132

Date	Events
1833	
1881	Statue to Morgan erected in Spartanburg, SC
1973	Daniel Morgan House ("Saratoga") near Winchester, Virginia becomes a National Historic Landmark
2013	Daniel Morgan House ("Saratoga") near Winchester, Virginia is added to the National Register of Historic Places

Daniel Morgan is one of the forgotten generals of the American Revolution, but his role was significant. He was a key part of the Colonial Army victory at Saratoga, and he personally led the Colonials at the huge victory at Cowpens in South Carolina. He served in all three major theaters of the War – With Arnold in Quebec, with Gates at Saratoga, with Washington in New Jersey, and under Gates and Green in the South. He was also a prisoner of war, captured at the Battle of Quebec.

His masterpiece was the Battle of Cowpens on January 17, 1781, when he destroyed the force under Banastre Tarleton. Below is Morgan's own report on the battle:

Camp near Cain Creek, Jan. 19,1781.

Dear Sir: The troops I have the honor to command have gained a complete victory over a detachment from the British army commanded by Lieut. Col. Tarleton. The action happened on the 17th inst., about sunrise, at a place called the Cowpens, near Pacolet river.

On the 14th, having received certain information that the British army were in motion, and that their movements clearly indicated their intentions of dislodging us, I abandoned my encampment at Grindale's Ford, and on the 16th, in the evening, took possession of a post about seven miles from the Cherokee Ford on Broad river. My former position subjected me at once to the operations of Lord Cornwallis and Colonel Tarleton, and in case of a defeat, my retreat might easily have been cut off. My situation at the Cowpens enabled me to improve any advantages I might gain, and to provide better for my own security, should I be unfortunate. These reasons induced me to take this post, notwithstanding it had the appearance of a retreat. On the evening of the 16th, the enemy occupied the ground we removed from in the morning. An hour before daylight, one of my scouts informed me that they had advanced within five miles of our camp. On this information, the necessary dispositions were made; and from the alacrity of the troops, we were soon prepared to receive them.

The light infantry, commanded by Lieut. Col. Howard, and the Virginia militia, under Major Triplett, were formed on a rising ground. The third regiment of dragoons, consisting of eighty men under the command of Lieut. Col. Washington, were so posted in their rear as not to be injured by the enemy's fire, and yet be able to charge the enemy, should an occasion offer. The volunteers from North Carolina, South Carolina and Georgia, under the command of Col. Pickens, were posted to guard the flanks. Major McDowell, of the North Carolina volunteers, was posted on the right flank, in front of the line one hundred and fifty yards, and Major Cunningham, of the Georgia volunteers, on the left, at the same distance in front. Colonels Brenner and Thomas, of the South Carolinians, on the right of Major McDowell, and Col. Hays and McCall, of the same corps, on the left of Major Cunningham. Captains Tate and Buchannan with the Augusta riflemen were to support the right of the line. The enemy drew up in one line four hundred yards in front of our advanced corps. The 1st battalion of the 71st regiment was opposed to our right; the 7th regiment to our left; the legion infantry to our centre, and two light companies, one hundred men each, on the flanks. In their front moved on two field pieces, and Lieut. Col. Tarleton with two hundred and eighty cavalry, was posted in the rear of his line. The disposition being thus made, small parties of riflemen were detached to skirmish with the enemy, on which their whole line advanced on with the greatest impetuosity, shouting as they advanced. Majors McDowell and Cunningham gave them a heavy fire and retreated to the regiments intended for their support. The whole of Col. Pickens's command then kept up a fire by regiments, retreating agreeable to their orders. When the enemy advanced to our line, they received a well directed and incessant fire; but their numbers being superior to ours, they gained our flanks, which obliged us to change our position. We retreated in good order about fifty paces, formed, advanced on the enemy and gave them a brisk fire, which threw them into disorder. Lieut. Colonel Howard observing this, gave orders for the line to charge bayonets, which was done with such address that the enemy fled with the utmost precipitation. Lieut. Colonel Washington discovering that the cavalry were cutting down our riflemen on the left, charged them with such firmness as obliged them to retire in confusion. The enemy were entirely routed, and the pursuit continued for upwards of twenty miles.

Our loss is very inconsiderable, not having more than twelve killed and sixty wounded. The enemy's loss was ten commissioned officers killed, and upwards of one hundred rank and file; two hundred wounded; twenty-nine commissioned officers and more than five hundred privates, prisoners, which fell into our hands, with two field pieces, two standards, eight hundred muskets, one travelling forge, thirty-five wagons, seventy negroes, and upwards of one hundred dragoon horses, and all their music. They destroyed most of their baggage, which was immense. Although our success was complete, we fought only eight hundred men, and were opposed by upwards of one thousand chosen British troops.

Such was the inferiority of our numbers, that our success must be attributed to the justice of our cause and the gallantry of our troops. My wishes would induce me to name every sentinel in the corps. In justice to the bravery and good conduct of the officers, I hare taken the liberty to enclose you a list of their names, from a conviction that you will be pleased to introduce such characters to the world.

Major Giles, my aid-de-camp, and Captain Brookes, my brigade major, deserve and have my thanks for their assistance and behavior on this occasion. The Baron de Glaebeut, who accompanies Major Giles with these dispatches, served with me as a volunteer, and behaved so as to merit your attention.

I am, dear Sir,
Your obedient servant,
Daniel Morgan.[65]

---

[65] *The Life of General Daniel Morgan*, by James Graham (Derby & Jackson, 1856)

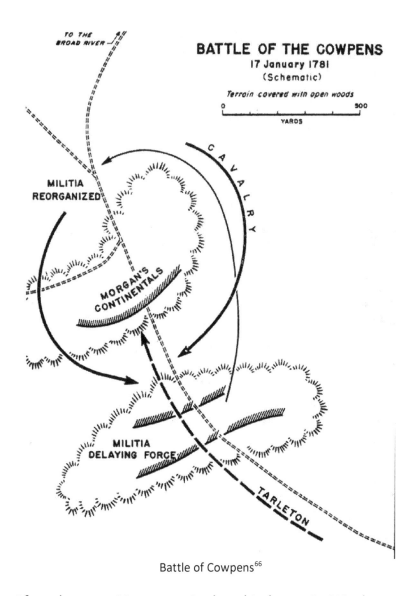

BATTLE OF THE COWPENS
17 January 1781
(Schematic)

Battle of Cowpens[66]

After the war, Morgan retired to his home in Winchester, Virginia, which he called "Saratoga", in honor of the great Colonial victory there. In 1790, he was awarded a gold medal by the Congress for his victory at Cowpens. The medal came accompanied by a letter from President George Washington.

---

[66] Public Domain. United States Army Center of Military History.

New You, March 25th, 1790.

Sir: You will receive with this a medal, struck by order of the late Congress, in commemoration of your much approved conduct in the battle of the Cowpens, and presented to you as a mark of the high sense which your country entertains of your services on that occasion.

This medal was put into my hands by Mr. Jefferson, and it is with singular pleasure that I now transmit it to you.

I am, Sir, &c., GEORGE WASHINGTON. [67]

In 1794, Morgan was briefly called back to service to lead troops in the Whiskey rebellion in Western Pennsylvania.

From March 4, 1797 – March 3, 1799, he served as a Congressman from Virginia.

"Portrait of Daniel Morgan, American general in the American Revolutionary War"[68]

---

[67] *The Life of General Daniel Morgan*, by James Graham (Derby & Jackson, 1856)
[68] By Charles Willson Peale (1741–1827). Independence National Historical Park. Public domain.

Thomas Paine

Date	Events
February 9, 1737	Born in Thetford, Norfolk, Great Britain
1744/49	Attends Thetford Grammar School
September 27, 1759	Marries Mary Lambert (she would die in labor in 1760)
1761/68	Various jobs as an Excise Officer, and also in the family business of making ropes for ships
March 26, 1771	Marries Elizabeth Ollive
1772	Publishes *The Case of the Officers of Excise*, calling for higher pay for excise officers
June 4, 1774	Separates from his wife and moves to London. He meets Benjamin Franklin.
October 1774	On Franklin's recommendation, Paine emigrates to America
January 1775	Becomes editor of the *Pennsylvania Magazine*
1776/83	Publishes a series of revolutionary tracts, entitled *The American Crisis*. "These are the times that try men's souls: The summer soldier and the sunshine patriot will, in this crisis, shrink from the service of their country; but he that stands it now, deserves the love and thanks of man and woman."
1776	Serves under George Washington
January 10, 1776	Publishes *Common Sense* anonymously
December 1776	The first tract of *The American Crisis* is published
1777	Three numbers of *The American Crisis* are published
April 17, 1777	Paine becomes secretary of the Congressional Committee on Foreign Affairs (continues until 1779)
1778	Three numbers of *The American Crisis* are published
c. 1780	Clerk to the Pennsylvania State Legislature
1780	• Three numbers of *The American Crisis* are published • Writes *Public Good* on the claim of Virginia to Western territory

Date	Events
March 1781	Fund raising expedition to France. He returns with 6,000,000 *livres* in silver, and a loan for 10,000,000 *livres*.
1782	Three numbers of *The American Crisis* are published
1783	• Purchases a home in Bordentown City, New Jersey • Two numbers of *The American Crisis* are published
1784	The New York State Legislature grants Paine a cottage and 320 acres in recognition of his services in the Revolutionary War
August 1785	After urging from George Washington, Paine is granted $3,000 for his services during the Revolution
1786	Writes *Dissertations on Government, the affairs of the Bank, and Paper Money*
1787	Designs the Schuylkill River Bridge in Philadelphia
April 1787	Travels to France, and displays his bridge model to the Academy of Sciences
September 1787	Travels to London
1788	Publishes *Prospects on the Rubicon* in England, about the difficulties between France and the United States on the one side, and Prussia on the other
March 1791	Publishes the first part of *Rights of Man* in England
February 1792	Publishes the second part of *Rights of Man* in England
September 1792	Elected to the French National Convention
December 1792	Tried *in absentia* in England for certain "seditious and libellous" passages in *Rights of Man*
December 1793	Arrested in Paris (Robespierre considered him an enemy). He was released in November 1794.
1793/94	Publishes *The Age of Reason*, a polemical against organized religion and Christianity (Paine was a Deist)
1795	Publishes *Agrarian Justice*, in which he argued for a guaranteed minimum income
April 1796	Writes *On the English System of Finance*

Date	Events
July 1796	Writes a nasty open *Letter to Washington*. Paine thought that Washington had conspired with Robespierre to have Paine imprisoned.
December 1797	Writes *Observations on the Construction and Operation of Navies with a Plan for an Invasion of England and the Final Overthrow of the English Government*
1800	He meets with Napoleon, who is a fan of *Rights of Man*
October 30, 1802	Returns to the United States
1803/05	Writes *An Essay on the Origin of Free-Masonry*
1804	Writes *To the People of England on the Invasion of England*
1811	Venezuelan translator Manuel Garcia de Sena translates some of Paine's works into Spanish
1835	Abraham Lincoln writes a defense of Thomas Paine's deism; it is soon destroyed by an associate
1839	A 12 foot marble column in honor of Paine is erected in New Rochelle, New York
June 8, 1809	Dies in New York City. Only six people came to his funeral.
1969	A 40 cent stamp honoring Thomas Paine is released by the United States Post Office
2002	Voted #34 of the one hundred greatest Britons

Thomas Paine, born in England in 1737, was a poor excise officer, a poor rope manufacturer, and one of the most brilliant and prolific political writers of his time. The change came in October 1774 when, on the advice of Benjamin Franklin, Paine abandoned his failed careers and failed marriage in England, and emigrated to the new world. Several of his works are still well known today.

On January 10, 1776, Paine published *Common Sense* anonymously. It immediately became a huge hit. It was divided into four parts.

Common Sense:
Addressed to the Inhabitants of America, on the Following Interesting Subjects, viz.
1. Of the Origin and Design of Government In general; With Concise Remarks on the English Constitution.
2. Of Monarchy And Hereditary Succession.
3. Thoughts On The Present State Of American Affairs.
4. Of The Present Ability of America; With Some Miscellaneous Reflections.

Thomas Paine by Auguste Millière (1880)[69]

It is perhaps the most pure philosophical discussion on why authoritative government is wrong, and government by the people is right. An example can be found below, from the *Of Monarchy And Hereditary Succession*, explaining why government by monarchy is invalid. So, Paine wasn't simply

---

[69] National Portrait Gallery: NPG 897. Public domain.

writing for American independence, he was invalidating the whole form of government in England!

> Government by kings was first introduced into the world by the Heathens, from whom the children of Israel copied the custom. It was the most prosperous invention the Devil ever set on foot for the promotion of idolatry...
>
> As the exalting one man so greatly above the rest cannot be justified on the equal rights of nature, so neither can it be defended on the authority of scripture; for the will of the Almighty as declared by Gideon, and the prophet Samuel, expressly disapproves of government by Kings...
>
> Even the distance at which the Almighty hath placed England and America is a strong and natural proof that the authority of the one over the other, was never the design of Heaven. The time likewise at which the Continent was discovered, adds weight to the argument, and the manner in which it was peopled, increases the force of it. The Reformation was preceded by the discovery of America: As if the Almighty graciously meant to open a sanctuary to the persecuted in future years, when home should afford neither friendship nor safety.
>
> But where says some is the King of America? I'll tell you Friend, he reigns above, and doth not make havoc of mankind like the Royal Brute of Britain... (*Common Sense* by Thomas Paine)[70]

During the war, from 1776/83, Paine published a series of revolutionary tracts, entitled *The American Crisis* (sometimes referred to simply as *The Crisis*. These tracts boosted morale of the Colonial troops and citizenry, and kept reminding them of what they were fighting for. Washington often had the tracts read to his men, including the beginning of the first tract in 1776:

> **THESE are the times that try men's souls. The summer soldier and the sunshine patriot will, in this crisis, shrink from the service of his country; but he that stands it NOW, deserves the**

---

[70] *Brief Sketch of the Life of Thomas Paine*, (Solomon King, 1830)

love and thanks of man and woman. Tyranny, like hell, is not easily conquered; yet we have this consolation with us, that the harder the conflict, the more glorious the triumph. What we obtain too cheap, we esteem too lightly: 'tis dearness only that gives every thing its value. Heaven knows how to put a proper price upon its goods; and it would be strange indeed, if so celestial an article as Freedom should not be highly rated. Britain, with an army to enforce her tyranny, has declared that she has a right (not only to Tax) but "to Bind Us in All Cases WhatSoever," and if being bound in that manner, is not slavery, then is there not such a thing as slavery upon earth. Even the expression is impious, for so unlimited a power can belong only to God.

Whether the independence of the continent was declared too soon, or delayed too long, I will not now enter into as an argument; my own simple opinion is, that had it been eight months earlier, it would have been much better. We did not make a proper use of last winter, neither could we, while we were in a dependent state. However, the fault, if it were one, was all our own; we have none to blame but ourselves. But no great deal it lost yet; all that Howe has been doing for this month past, is rather a ravage than a conquest, which the spirit of the Jerseys a year ago would have quickly repulsed, and which time and a little resolution will soon recover.[71] (emphasis added)

In 1776, Paine briefly served as an aide to General George Washington, and on April 17, 1777, Paine became secretary of the Congressional Committee on Foreign Affairs, a post that he maintained until 1779.

In August 1785, at the urging of George Washington, Paine was granted $3,000 for his services during the Revolution from the Congress of the United States.

Resolved, that the early, unsolicited, and continued labors of Mr. Thomas Paine, in explaining and enforcing the principles of the late revolution, by ingenious and timely publications upon the nature of liberty and civil government, have been well received by the citizens of these states, and merit the approbation of

---

[71] *Brief Sketch of the Life of Thomas Paine*, (Solomon King, 1830)

congress; and that in consideration of these services, and the benefits produced thereby, Mr. Paine is entitled to a liberal gratification from the United States.[72]

After the war, many of his former admirers soured on him, because of his publication in 1793/94 of *The Age of Reason*, a polemical against organized religion and Christianity (Paine was a Deist), and his perhaps too-close association with the French revolution, which was not altogether approved of in the United States. However, Paine will always be remembered for his pamphlets and tracts which provided the rallying cry for the American Revolution.

---

[72] *Brief Sketch of the Life of Thomas Paine*, (Solomon King, 1830)

Paul Revere

Portrait of Paul Revere by John Singleton Copley[73]

Date	Events
January 1, 1735	Born in North End, Boston, Massachusetts (3rd of 12 children)
1748	Apprentices in his father's silversmith shop
1754	Death of Revere's father
February 1756	Enlists in the army during the French and Indian War as a second lieutenant in an artillery regiment. He would serve at Fort William Henry.
August 4, 1757	Marries Sarah Orne (d. 1773). They would have 8

[73] Public domain. Museum of Fine Arts Boston.

Date	Events
	children.
1765	Revere joins the "Sons of Liberty"
1768	Produces an engraving of British troops arriving in Boston
March 1770	Produces an engraving of the Boston Massacre
1770	Revere purchases a home on North Square in North End, Boston
October 10, 1773	Marries Rachel Walker. They would have 8 children.
December 16, 1773	Participates in the Boston Tea Party
December 1773 - November 1775	Courier for the Boston Committee of Public Safety, riding to New York City and Philadelphia
1774	• Contributes engravings to the *Royal American Magazine* • Attends secret meetings with fellow patriots at the the *Green Dragon*, after General Gage moves troops into Boston, and issues a decree that they be billeted with private citizens
December 1774	Rides to Portsmouth, New Hampshire on rumors that the British had landed nearby
April 7, 1775	Revere sent to Concord by Joseph Warren to warn the Massachusetts Provincial Congress of British troop movements
April 18, 1775	Midnight Ride of Paul Revere
November 1775	Sent by the Provincial Congress to Philadelphia to study the workings of a powder mill there. The information he gleaned there allowed Revere to open a powder mill in Stoughton (Canton) – south of Boston
1775	Revere writes of his Midnight Ride in a deposition to the Massachusetts Provincial Congress. The Congress wanted to establish that the British fired first.
March 21, 1776	Revere and the brothers of Joseph Warren retrieve Warren's body from a shallow grave at Bunker Hill, and give it a proper burial in a marked grave
April 1776	Commissioned a major of infantry in the

Date	Events
	Massachusetts militia (he soon transferred to artillery)
November 1776	Promoted to lieutenant colonel, and stationed at Castle William, defending Boston harbor
August 1777	Escorts prisoners taken in the Battle of Bennington (August 16, 1777) to Boston
August 1778	Commands an artillery unit on Aquidneck Island as part of the American/French actions which led to the Battle of Rhode Island
July 24, 1779 – August 14, 1779	Commands artillery unit during the abortive Penobscot Expedition in Maine
February 1782	Revere is absolved of any wrong doing for his actions during the Penobscot Expedition
1788	Constructs a large furnace for metal, and then an iron furnace
1792	New business: church bell casting, with the company Paul Revere & Sons
1794	Begins cannon casting
1795	Copper casting for naval purposes (spikes, bolts)
July 4, 1795	Representing the grand lodge of Freemasons in Massachusetts, Revere and Governor Samuel Adams place items in the cornerstone of the Massachusetts State House
1798	Paul Revere writes a letter to Jeremy Belknap, founder of the Massachusetts Historical Society describing his Midnight Ride
1801	Founds Revere Copper Company to roll copper into sheets for use as sheathing on naval vessels. The Revere Copper Company still exists today.
1802	Copper from Revere Copper Company covers the dome on the Massachusetts State House
May 10, 1818	Dies in Boston, Massachusetts. He is buried in the Granary Burying Ground on Tremont Street.
1861	Henry Wadsworth Longfellow writes the poem *Paul Revere's Ride*
1871	Revere, Massachusetts is so named
1958	25 cent stamp honoring Paul Revere is issued by the Post Office
1960s	*Paul Revere and the Raiders* are a popular rock

147

Date	Events
group	

Paul Revere was a silversmith, Revolutionary War officer and courier, and an early Industrial Revolution pioneer. He was a member of the *Sons of Liberty* in Boston, and a participant in the Boston Tea Party of 1773.

Revere got his first war experience serving as a second lieutenant in an artillery regiment during the French and Indian War. He served at Fort William Henry. In the Revolutionary War, he was commissioned a major of infantry in the Massachusetts militia in April 1776. He soon transferred to artillery. Promoted to lieutenant colonel in November 1776, he was stationed at Castle William, defending Boston harbor. He saw field action in August 1778 when he commanded an artillery unit on Aquidneck Island as part of the American/French actions which led to the Battle of Rhode Island.

His most controversial military service occurred during the ill-fated Penobscot Expedition in Maine, July 24, 1779 – August 14, 1779, when he commanded an artillery unit. In this unmitigated disaster of an operation (the whole naval fleet sent by the Colonials was destroyed), enemies of Revere tried to make him the scapegoat. Revere demanded a formal court-martial, and in February 1782 he was absolved of any wrong doing for his actions during the Penobscot Expedition.

Revere, of course, is best known in American history as a courier. He first acted in this capacity for the Boston Committee of Public Safety from December 1773 - November 1775, when he would ride to New York City and Philadelphia. He may have made up to 18 "rides" during this period.

In December 1774, he rode to Portsmouth, New Hampshire on (untrue) rumors that the British had landed nearby. On April 7, 1775, Revere was sent to Concord by Joseph Warren to warn the Massachusetts Provincial Congress of British troop movements.

And then, on Tuesday evening, April 18, 1775, Revere made a midnight ride from Boston to Charlestown, Medford and Lexington. Revere was captured between Lexington and Concord. Also making midnight rides that night: William Dawes (the southern route, via Cambridge) and Dr. Samuel Prescott, who joined them in Lexington.

We actually have Paul Revere's own account of his famous Midnight Ride. It was recorded in a letter to Dr. Jeremy Belknap, founder of the Massachusetts Historical Society in 1798.

On Tuesday evening, the 18th, it was observed that a number of soldiers were marching towards the bottom of the Common. About 10 o'clock, Dr. [Joseph] Warren sent in great haste for me and begged that I would immediately set off for Lexington, where Messrs. Hancock and Adams were, and acquaint them of the movement, and that it was thought they were the objects.

When I got to Dr. Warren's house, I found he had sent an express by land to Lexington — a Mr. William Daws [Dawes]. The Sunday before, by desire of Dr. Warren, I had been to Lexington, to Messrs. Hancock and Adams, who were at the Rev. Mr. Clark's. I returned at night through Charlestown; there I agreed with a Colonel [William] Conant and some other gentlemen that if the British went out by water, we would show two lanthorns [lanterns] in the North Church steeple; and if by land, one, as a signal; for we were apprehensive it would be difficult to cross the Charles River or get over Boston Neck. I left Dr. Warren, called upon a friend and desired him to make the signals.

I then went home ... went to the north part of the town, where I had kept a boat; two friends rowed me across Charles River, a little to the eastward where the man-of-war Somerset lay. It was then young flood, the ship was winding, and the moon was rising. They landed me on the Charlestown side. When I got into town, I met Colonel Conant and several others; they said they had seen our signals. I told them what was acting, and went to get me a horse; I got a horse of Deacon Larkin. While the horse was preparing, Richard Devens, Esq., who was one of the Committee of Safety, came to me and told me that he came down the road from Lexington after sundown that evening; that he met ten British officers, all well mounted, and armed, going up the road.

I set off upon a very good horse; it was then about eleven o'clock and very pleasant. After I had passed Charlestown Neck... I saw two men on horseback under a tree. When I got near them, I discovered they were British officers. One tried to get ahead of me, and the other to take me. I turned my horse very quick and galloped towards Charlestown Neck, and then pushed for the Medford Road. The one who chased me, endeavoring to cut me off, got into a clay pond near where Mr. Russell's Tavern is now built. I got clear of him, and went through Medford, over the bridge and up to Menotomy. In Medford, I awaked the captain of the minute men; and after that, I alarmed almost every house, till got to Lexington. I found Messers Hancock and Adams at the Rev. Mr. Clark's; I told them my errand and enquired for Mr. Daws; they said he had not been there; I related the story of the two officers, and supposed that he must have been stopped, as he ought to have been there before me.

After I had been there about half an hour, Mr. Daws came; we refreshed ourselves, and set off for Concord. We were overtaken by a young Dr. Prescott, whom we found to be a high Son of Liberty. I told them of the ten officers that Mr. Devens met, and that it was probable we might be stopped before we got to Concord; for I supposed that after night they divided themselves, and that two of them had fixed themselves in such passages as were most likely to stop any intelligence going to Concord. I likewise mentioned that we had better alarm all the inhabitants till we got to Concord. The young doctor much approved of it and said he would stop with either of us, for the people between that and Concord knew him and would give the more credit to what we said.

We had got nearly half way. Mr. Daws and the doctor stopped to alarm the people of a house. I was about one hundred rods ahead when I saw two men in nearly the same situation as those officers were near Charlestown. I called for the doctor and Mr. Daws to come up. In an instant I was surrounded by four. They had placed themselves in a straight road that inclined each way; they had taken down a pair of bars on the north side of the road, and two of them were under a tree in the pasture. The doctor being foremost, he came up and we tried to get past them; but they being armed with pistols and swords, they forced us into the pasture. The doctor jumped his horse over a low stone wall and got to Concord.

I observed a wood at a small distance and made for that. When I got there, out started six officers on horseback and ordered me to dismount. One of them, who appeared to have the command, examined me, where I came from and what my name was. I told him. He asked me if I was an express [messenger]. I answered in the affirmative. He demanded what time I left Boston. I told him, and added that their troops had catched aground in passing the river, and that there would be five hundred Americans there in a short time, for I had alarmed the country all the way up. He immediately rode towards those who stopped us, when all five of them came down upon a full gallop. One of them, whom I afterwards found to be a Major Mitchel, of the 5th Regiment, clapped his pistol to my head, called me by name and told me he was going to ask me some questions, and if I did not give him true answers, he would blow my brains out. He then asked me similar questions to those above. He then ordered me to mount my horse, after searching me for arms. He then ordered them to advance and to lead me in front. When we got to the road, they turned down towards Lexington. When we had all got about one mile, the major rode up to the officer who was leading me and told him to give me to the sergeant. As soon as he took me, the major ordered him, if I attempted to run, or anybody insulted them, to blow my brains out.

We rode till we got near Lexington meeting-house, when the militia fired a volley of guns, which appeared to alarm them very much. The major inquired of me how far it was to Cambridge, and if there were any other road. After some consultation, the Major rode up to the Sargent, & asked if his Horse was tired? He told answered him, he was - (He was a Sargent of Grenadiers, and had a small Horse) - then, said he, take that man's horse. I dismounted, & the Sargent mounted my Horse, when they all rode towards Lexington Meeting-House. I went across the Burying-ground, & some pastures, and came to the Rev. Mr. Clark's house, where I found Messrs. Hancock and Adams. I told them of my treatment, and they concluded to go from that house towards Woburn. I went with them, & a Mr. Lowell, who was a Clerk to Mr. Hancock. When we got to the house where they intended to stop, Mr. Lowell & I my self returned to Mr. Clark's, to find what was going on. When we got there, an elderly man came in; he said he had just come from the Tavern, that a man had come from Boston, who said there were no British troops coming. Mr. Lowell & myself went towards the Tavern, when we met a man on a full gallop, who told us the troops were coming up the Rocks. We afterwards met another, who said they were close by. Mr. Lowell asked me to go to the Tavern with him, to [get] a trunk of papers belonging to Mr. Hancock...while we were getting the trunk, we saw the British very near, upon a full march. We hurried towards Mr. Clark's house. In our way we passed through the militia. There were about fifty. When we had got about one hundred yards from the meeting-house, the British troops appeared on both sides of the meeting-house. In their Front was an Officer on horse back. They made a Short Halt; when I saw, & heard, a gun fired which appeared to be a pistol. Then I could distinguish two guns, and then a continual roar of musketry; when we made off with the trunk...[74]

After the War, Revere expanded his silversmith business, and began working in iron, bronze and copper. He built furnaces and forges, manufacturing church bells, copper sheeting, copper spikes and bolts for naval use and cannons. One of the companies he founded, Revere Copper Company is still in business today.

In 1861, Revere was immortalized in Henry Wadsworth Longfellow's poem *Paul Revere's Ride*, which got some of the bits correct. An excerpt is below:

Listen my children and you shall hear

---

[74] Public domain. http://www.masshist.org/database/99

Of the midnight ride of Paul Revere,
On the eighteenth of April, in Seventy-five;
Hardly a man is now alive
Who remembers that famous day and year.

He said to his friend, "If the British march
By land or sea from the town to-night,
Hang a lantern aloft in the belfry arch
Of the North Church tower as a signal light,--
One if by land, and two if by sea;
And I on the opposite shore will be,
Ready to ride and spread the alarm
Through every Middlesex village and farm,
For the country folk to be up and to arm."[75]

Revolutionary War hero and manufacturer extraordinaire, Paul Revere left his mark on the early days of the American Republic.

Baron Friedrich von Steuben

> I should do injustice if I were to be longer silent with regard to the merits of the baron De Steuben. His knowledge of his profession, added to the zeal which he has discovered since he began upon the functions of his office, lead me to consider him as an acquisition to the service, and to recommend him to the attention of Congress. His expectations with regard to rank extend to that of major-general. His finances, he ingenuously confesses, will not admit of his serving without the incident emoluments; and Congress, I presume, from his character and their own knowledge of him, will without difficulty gratify him in these particulars.[76] (George Washington)

If one is looking for the hand of Providence in the victory of the colonists over Britain, one might see it in the person of Baron von Steuben (b. 1739; d. 1794), a former Prussian military officer who showed up at Valley Forge at the very time that Washington had an urgent need to train his undisciplined troops. Valley Forge, which could have been an unmitigated disaster for Washington and his troops, ended up being a valuable interlude in which Washington's army received necessary training, thanks to von Steuben.

Date	Events
September 17, 1730	Born in Magdeburg, Duchy of Magdeburg
1747	Joins Prussian Army
May 6, 1757	Wounded in the Battle of Prague
1758	Adjutant to General Johann von Mayer
1759	• Promoted to first lieutenant • Wounded at Battle of Kunersdorf
June 26, 1761	Deputy quartermaster at headquarters
1761	Taken prisoner at Treptow
1762	• Released from prison

---

[76] *Official Letters to the Honorable American Congress*, by George Washington (Cadell Junior and Davies, 1795)

154

Date	Events
	• Promoted to Captain • Aide-de-camp to Frederick the Great
April 29, 1763	Discharged from the Prussian Army after a peace agreement was signed (Seven Years War)
1764/77	Chamberlain to Fürst Josef Friedrich Wilhelm of Hohenzollern-Hechingen
May 26, 1769	Awarded the Star of the Order of Fidelity by the Duchess of Wurttemburg (niece of Frederick the Great)
1771	Receives title of Baron (probably from Fürst Josef Friedrich Wilhelm of Hohenzollern-Hechingen)
1777	Meets with French Minister of War, Claude Louis, Comte de Saint-Germain, who introduces von Steuben to Benjamin Franklin; Franklin writes a letter of introduction to George Washington
February 5, 1778	Meets with Continental Congress in York, Pennsylvania; he is mistakenly introduced as Lieutenant General von Steuben (*Lieutenant General Quarters Maitre*, which really meant deputy quartermaster)
February 23, 1778	Reports to Washington at Valley Forge, and soon begins training the troops
April 30, 1778	Washington nominates von Steuben as inspector general, which is approved by Congress on May 5, 1778
Winter 1778/79	Authors *Regulations for the Order and Discipline of the Troops of the United States* (Revolutionary War Drill Manual)
1781	Travels with Nathanael Greene to Virginia as part of the Southern Campaign
September 28 – October 19, 1781	Leads a division at Yorktown
March 24, 1783	Discharged from the military with honors
December 23, 1783	Presented by the State of New Jersey with use of the Zabriskie-Steuben House, which had been seized from a loyalist two years before. Five years later, the house was given to von Steuben.
March 1784	Made a citizen of the United States by the

155

Date	Events
	Pennsylvania legislature
November 28, 1794	Dies in Utica, New York
1795	Steubenville, Ohio is founded
June 9, 1917	Captured German ship *SS Kronprinz Wilhelm* is renamed *USS Von Steuben* by the United States, and used as a troop ship
1919	Steuben Society is founded
1928	The cadet barracks at Valley Forge Military Academy is named in honor of von Steuben
June 27, 1928	The State of New Jersey purchases the Steuben House, which today is administered by the Historic New Bridge Landing Park Commission
1930	General Von Steuben stamp issued by the U.S. Post Office
September 30, 1964	Nuclear submarine *USS Von Steuben* is commissioned
1958 - Annually	German-American Steuben Parade held in various locations in America. In New York City, the parade is held in September.
1979	Portrayed by Nehemiah Persoff in the miniseries *The Rebels*
1984	Portrayed by Kurt Knudson in the miniseries *George Washington*

In 1778, von Steuben authored *Regulations for the Order and Discipline of the Troops of the United States* (*Revolutionary War Drill Manual*), which became the standard training manual for the U.S. Army until the War of 1812. Some excerpts follow.

CHAP. XVI. The manner of laying out a Camp, with the order of Encampment.
WHEN the quarter-masters arrive on the ground where the troops are to encamp, the quarter-master-general having fixed his line of encampment, will conduct them along the line, and give each brigade-quarter-master the ground necessary for his brigade.

The quarter-masters of regiments will then have their ground given them by the brigade-quarter-masters, and will mark out the place for each company and tent, and for the kitchens, &c. &c... The infantry will on all occasions encamp by battalions, as they are formed in order of battle.

The front of a camp will occupy the same extent of ground as the troops when formed; and the intervals between the battalions wilt be twenty paces, with an addition of eight paces for every piece of cannon a battalion may have.

The quarter-master of each regiment shall be answerable that he demands no more ground than is necessary for the number of men he has actually with the regiment, allowing two feet for each file, exclusive of the officers, and adding sixteen feet for the intervals between the platoons. He is also to be answerable that no more tents are pitched than are absolutely necessary, allowing one tent for the non-commissioned officers of each company, and one for every six men, including the drums and fifes.

The tents of the non-commissioned officers and privates are to be pitched in two ranks, with an interval of six paces between the ranks, and two feet between each tent: the tents of the non-commissioned officers to be in the front rank on the right of their companies, in the right wing, and on the left in the left wing of the battalion. Nine feet front are to be allowed for each tent with its interval, and twenty feet in the centre of the battalion for the adjutant; but when a regiment forms two battalions, the adjutant is to encamp with the first battalion, the sergeant-major supplying his place in the second.

The captains' and subalterns' tents are to be in one line, twenty feet from the rear of the men's tents; the captains' in the right wing opposite the right of their respective companies, and the subalterns' opposite the left; and the contrary in the left wing.

The field officers' tents are to be in one line, thirty feet from the line of officers; the colonel's opposite the centre; the lieutenant-colonel's on the right; and the major's on the left. But if the regiment forms two battalions, the colonel encamps behind the centre of the first battalion: the lieutenant-colonel behind the second battalion: and the major behind the interval between the two battalions.

The surgeon, pay-master and quarter-master encamp in one line, with the front of their tents in a line with the rear of the field officers' tents; the surgeon on the right, pay-master on the left, and quarter-master in the centre.

The kitchens are to be dug behind their respective companies, forty feet from the field officers' tents. The settlers' tents are to be between the kitchens.

The horses and wagons are to be placed in a line, twenty feet behind the kitchens.

The drums of each battalion are to be piled six paces in front of the adjutant's tent, and the colours planted before them.

The camp guards are to be three hundred paces in front of the first line, and the same distance in the rear of the second line.

The quarter guard is to be forty feet from the waggons, opposite the interval between the two battalions who furnish it.
The sinks of the first line are to be three hundred feet in front, and those of the second line the same distance in the rear of the camp.

The commanding officers of regiments are to be answerable that no tents are pitched out of the line of encampment, on any account whatever, except for the regimental hospital.

The ground being marked out, the quarter-masters will leave the pioneers, and go to meet their regiments, conduct them to their ground, and inform the colonel where they are, to go for their necessaries.[77]

---

[77] *Steuben's Regulations for the Order and Discipline of the Troops of the United States*, by Friedrich Wilhelm Ludolf Gerhard Augustin Baron von Steuben (Printed for William Pelham, 1807)

"Major General Friedrich Wilhelm Augustus, Baron von Steuben", 1786[78]

Baron von Steuben drilling Washington's army at Valley Forge[79]

---

[78] Public domain. Yale University Art Gallery.
[79] Library of Congress http://www.loc.gov/pictures/item/2002725153/

Baron von Steuben also served as inspector general of Washington's army, and served in the Southern campaign with Nathanael Greene. von Steuben led a division at the Battle of Yorktown.

George Washington

Date	Events
February 22, 1732	Born in Westmoreland, Virginia to Augustine Washington (1694/1743) and Mary Ball Washington (1708/89)
1743	Washington's father, Augustine Washington, dies; Washington inherits 10 slaves
1749	Thanks to the influence of the Fairfax family, Washington is appointed surveyor for Culpeper County
1751	Washington contracts smallpox on a trip to Barbados with his tubercular half-brother Lawrence
1752	Lawrence dies, leaving half of the Mount Vernon Estate to his brother George
February 1753	Governor Dinwiddie appoints Washington as one of the four district adjutants, a position once held by his brother Lawrence, with the rank of major in the Virginia militia
1752 or 1753	Washington joins the Freemasons
Late 1753	Washington is asked to deliver a letter by Governor Dinwiddie to the French in the Ohio Valley, ordering them to vacate; he delivers the letter to Jacques Legardeur de Saint-Pierre, who refuses to leave
1753/54	Washington's *Journal to the Ohio* is published with the backing of Governor Dinwiddie
1754/62	French and Indian War
May 28, 1754	Washington defeats the French under Joseph Coulon de Jumonville near Uniontown, Pennsylvania (south of Pittsburgh) in the Battle of Jumonville Glen; de Jumonville may have been killed by an Indian ally of the British
July 1754	Washington and his militia are captured at Fort Necessity, SE of Uniontown, Pennsylvania; Washington and his troops are allowed to return to Virginia
July 9, 1755	The British are routed by the French at the Battle of the Monongahela, near Braddock, Pennsylvania; Washington helps secure an orderly retreat

Date	Events
1755	Washington is appointed "Colonel of the Virginia Regiment and Commander in Chief of all forces now raised in the defense of His Majesty's Colony" by Governor Dinwiddie; Washington is assigned 1,000 soldiers to guard Virginia's border – they will fight in 20 battles
1758	• Washington is part of the Forbes Expedition to capture Fort Duquesne; 40 men are killed or wounded in a British friendly fire incident • Elected to the Virginia House of Burgesses
December 1758	Washington resigns from his Virginia Regiment commission
January 6, 1759	Marries widow Martha Dandridge Custis, and moves to Mount Vernon; the couple will not have any children
1765	Opposes the Stamp Act and the Townshend Acts (1767)
1766	Primary cash crop of Mount Vernon is switched to wheat from tobacco
1769/1770	Washington receives 23,000 acres in what is now West Virginia from the Virginia governor in thanks for his role in the French and Indian War; along with his wife's wealth, this makes Washington one of the richest plantation owners in Virginia
1774	Opposes the "Intolerable Acts", passed to punish the colonies after the Boston Tea Party
July 1774	Chairs a meeting calling for the convening of a Continental Congress
August 1774	Washington is selected as a delegate to the Continental Congress
1775	Mount Vernon is 6,500 acres in size
April 1775	Battles of Lexington and Concord
June 14, 1775	The Continental Congress creates the Continental Army. After being nominated by John Adams, Washington accepts the position of General and Commander-in-chief.
March 1776	Washington forces a British evacuation from Boston, after seizing the Dorchester Heights; Washington's army occupies New York City
August 27,	Washington is defeated in the Battle of Long Island

162

Date	Events
1776	(also known as the Battle of Brooklyn Heights) by William Howe; Washington evacuates New York City
December 25, 1776	Washington wins a stunning victory by crossing the Delaware River and capturing 900+ Hessian soldiers in Trenton
January 3, 1777	Victory at Princeton, New Jersey
September 11, 1777	Howe defeats Washington at Brandywine, Pennsylvania
September 26, 1777	Howe occupies Philadelphia
October 4, 1777	British defeat Washington at Germantown
October 17, 1777	Burgoyne defeated by Horatio Gates at the Battle of Saratoga (New York)
December 5-8, 1777	Battle of Whitemarsh, where Washington maintains the field
December 19, 1777	Washington's battered army arrives at Valley Forge, where they will be trained by ex-Prussian officer Baron Friedrich von Steuben
February 6, 1778	France enters into an alliance with the 13 colonies
March 7, 1778	British General William Howe is replaced by Henry Clinton
June 18, 1778	The British abandon Philadelphia, and retreat to New York City. Washington's troops march into Philadelphia the next day.
June 28, 1778	The British are driven from the field in the Battle of Monmouth, New Jersey
Summer 1779	Washington orders raids by General John Sullivan against British allies the Iroquois in upstate New York
July 1780	General Comte Donatien de Rochambeau leads 5,000 French troops into Rhode Island
February 1781	Daniel Morgan defeats Banastre Tarleton's army at Cowpens
October 19, 1781	Victory at Yorktown
September 3, 1783	Treaty of Paris officially ends the Revolutionary War

Date	Events
November 2, 1783	Washington bids farewell to his troops
November 25, 1783	British evacuate New York City
December 4, 1783	Washington formally bids farewell to his officers
December 23, 1783	Washington resigns as commander-in-chief
1784	Washington purchases his first set of false teeth (most were made from ivory; none from wood)
Summer 1787	Elected president of the Constitutional Convention in Philadelphia
1788	Becomes master of Alexandria Lodge No. 22
1789	Unanimous choice for president
April 30, 1789	Sworn in as president at Federal Hall in New York City
1790	Signs the Residence Act, which sets the stage for a permanent national capitol
1791	Washington in the Territory of Columbia is selected as the nation's capitol
1791/94	Whiskey Rebellion in Western Pennsylvania
1792	Unanimous choice for president
1792	Militia Act is passed by Congress, allowing Washington to call up state militias to suppress the Whiskey Rebellion. Washington would personally lead the troops (!)
1793	Washington declares United States neutrality in the War between France and England
November 19, 1794	Jay Treaty resolves left over issues from the Revolution, and opens trade with Great Britain
1796	Washington makes a large endowment to what is now called Washington and Lee University in Lexington, Virginia
September 19, 1796	Washington's Farewell Address ("The Address of General Washington To The People of The United States on his declining of the Presidency of the United States,") is first published
February 1797	Mount Vernon opens a distillery
July 4, 1798	President John Adams appoints Washington lieutenant general and Commander-in-chief of the

Date	Events
	armies, because of fear of a war with France
December 14, 1799	Dies in Mount Vernon, Virginia from severe respiratory distress, and probably aggravated by too-aggressive bloodletting. Martha Washington would soon burn almost all letters between her and her husband. Washington's will freed all of his slaves, an act which his widow Mary duplicated a year later.
December 18, 1799	Funeral at Mount Vernon
1800	The Territory of Columbia becomes the District of Columbia
February 9, 1821	George Washington University established in the nation's capitol
1846	Construction of the Washington Monument begins. After pausing for the Civil War, construction begins again in 1877, and is finished in 1884.
February 22, 1853	Washington University in St. Louis is established
1862	24 cent Washington stamp issued
1869	Washington first appears on the $1 bill
November 11, 1889	Washington state is admitted to the Union
1895	2 cent Washington stamp issued
1917	*886 Washingtonia asteroid* named
March 3, 1925	Enshrined on Mount Rushmore, South Dakota
1928	A 2 cent stamp of Washington at Prayer, Valley Forge is issued
1931	Battle of Yorktown stamp issued (2 cents), with General Rochambeau, Washington and Admiral DeGrasse pictured
1932	Washington first appears on the quarter
1937	A 3 cent stamp commemorating Washington as the president of the Constitutional Convention in 1787 is issued
1939	A 3 cent stamp commemorating Washington's presidential oath in 1789 is issued
1976	Various Bicentennial souvenir sheets are released, including "Washington reviewing his ragged army at Valley Forge", "The surrender of Lord Cornwallis at

165

Date	Events
	Yorktown", "Washington Crossing the Delaware"
July 4, 1976	George Washington appointed *General of the Armies of the United States* by the U.S. Congress (s:Public Law 94-479); "It is considered fitting and proper that no officer of the United States Army should outrank Lieutenant General George Washington on the Army list"
January 3, 1977	Battle of Princeton commemorative is issued
1981	Two stamps commemorating the Battle of Yorktown are issued
April 16, 1989	Bicentennial of the Executive Branch commemorative (25 cents) is issued at Mount Vernon

"The prayer at Valley Forge", c. 1866[80]

Looking back from the distance of 200+ years, it seems almost impossible that the 13 colonies were able to win a war against the most powerful nation on earth at the time, Great Britain. But win they did, and no person is owed a greater portion of

---

[80] Library of Congress   http://www.loc.gov/pictures/item/2009633684/

the plaudits than the Commander-in-Chief of the Continental Army, George Washington (b. 1732; d. 1799).

Washington's military career began in February 1753 when Virginia Governor Dinwiddie appointed Washington as one of the four district adjutants, a position once held by his brother Lawrence, with the rank of major in the Virginia militia. Later that same year, Washington was asked to deliver a letter by Governor Dinwiddie to the French in the Ohio Valley, ordering them to vacate. The letter was duly delivered, and the French refused to leave. This led to the initial stirrings of the French and Indian War.

On May 28, 1754, Washington defeated the French under Joseph Coulon de Jumonville near Uniontown, Pennsylvania (south of Pittsburgh) in the Battle of Jumonville Glen. Washington's fortunes would abruptly change two months later when, in July 1754, Washington and his militia were captured at Fort Necessity, southeast of Uniontown, Pennsylvania. Washington and his troops were soon allowed to return to Virginia.

On July 9, 1755, the British were routed by the French at the Battle of the Monongahela, near Braddock, Pennsylvania. Washington helped secure an orderly retreat.

Also in 1755, Washington was appointed "Colonel of the Virginia Regiment and Commander in Chief of all forces now raised in the defense of His Majesty's Colony" by Governor Dinwiddie. Washington was assigned 1,000 soldiers to guard Virginia's border – they would fight in 20 battles.

In 1758, Washington served as part of the Forbes Expedition to capture Fort Duquesne. During this operation, 40 men were killed or wounded in a British friendly fire incident. In

December 1758, Washington resigned from his Virginia Regiment commission.

On June 14, 1775, the Continental Congress created the Continental Army. After being nominated by John Adams, Washington accepted the position of General and Commander-in-chief. He would serve in this capacity for the rest of the war.

Like most generals, Washington's record as a battlefield commander had both its high and low points. Among the high points: Dorchester Heights, Trenton ("Washington Crosses the Delaware"), Princeton, Whitemarsh, Monmouth, and of course, Yorktown. Among the low points: the Battle of Long Island (also known as the Battle of Brooklyn Heights), Brandywine, Germantown, and the retreats from New York City and Philadelphia.

Washington's greatness as a general, though, does not rest solely on his performance on the battlefield. He accomplished the seemingly impossible task of keeping his ragtag army of untrained, undisciplined volunteers intact for two years until the French entered the war, while facing the greatest military machine in the world at the time. And he managed to get them trained along the way at Valley Forge.

Once Washington had the resources of the French army and (especially) navy, he was able to do what the English were unable to do to his army – have a decisive victory. The victory at Yorktown reverberates through history as one of the greatest and most important strategic battles. While one can't lessen the impact of the French navy in winning the battle, Yorktown was Washington's show, and he will forever be praised for it.

Washington also seemed adept at choosing subordinates. Leaving aside Charles Lee and Benedict Arnold, whose betrayals Washington couldn't have foreseen, Washington picked a pretty solid bunch of generals, including Nathanael Greene, Baron von Steuben, Marquis de Lafayette, "Mad" Anthony Wayne, and others. Lincoln took almost three years to finally find his generals; Washington chose the right ones at the start.

On December 4, 1783, Washington formally bid farewell to his officers, and on December 23, 1783, Washington resigned as commander-in-chief. This resignation shocked Europe, as no one with that much power had ever resigned before.

How does Washington compare with other great generals of American history, including Grant, Sherman, Lee, Pershing, Eisenhower, MacArthur and Patton? The Congress of the United States in 1976 passed a resolution that "no officer of the United States Army should outrank Lieutenant General George Washington". The Congress created the rank of "General of the Armies of the United States", and assigned it to Washington solely. Other generals (Grant, Sherman, Sheridan, Pershing) had the title "General of the Army", and during World War II, several men were promoted to five-star generals (George Marshall, Douglas MacArthur, Dwight D. Eisenhower, Henry H. "Hap" Arnold, Omar Bradley), but none would ever outrank Washington.

94TH UNITED STATES CONGRESS
2ND SESSION

Joint Resolution
to provide for the appointment of George Washington to the grade of General of the Armies of the United States.

Whereas Lieutenant General George Washington of Virginia commanded our armies throughout and to the successful termination of our Revolutionary War;

Whereas Lieutenant General George Washington presided over the convention that formulated our Constitution;

Whereas Lieutenant General George Washington twice served as President of the United States of America; and

Whereas it is considered fitting and proper that no officer of the United States Army should outrank Lieutenant General George Washington on the Army list: Now, therefore, be it

Resolved by the Senate and House of Representatives of the United States of America in Congress assembled, That
(a) for purposes of subsection (b) of this section only, the grade of General of the Armies of the United States is established, such grade to have rank and precedence over all other grades of the Army, past or present.
(b) The President is authorized and requested to appoint George Washington posthumously to the grade of General of the Armies of the United States, such appointment to take effect on July 4, 1976.

Approved October 11, 1976.[81]

In 1789, Washington was chosen unanimously as president, an honor repeated in 1792. He is the only U.S. President to ever be elected president unanimously.

In 1792 during the Whiskey Rebellion, Congress passed the Militia Act which allowed Washington to call up state militia. For the last time in his illustrious career, Washington would personally lead the troops.

On September 19, 1796, Washington published his Farewell Address (*The Address of General Washington To The People of*

---

[81] Public domain.   http://www.gpo.gov/fdsys/pkg/STATUTE-90/pdf/STATUTE-90-Pg2078.pdf

The United States on his Declining of the Presidency of the United States) after turning down the opportunity to stand for a third term. It contains the famous advice to avoid the "insidious wiles of foreign influence".

> ...a passionate attachment of one nation for another produces a variety of evils. Sympathy for the favorite nation, facilitating the illusion of an imaginary common interest in cases where no real common interest exists, and infusing into one the enmities of the other, betrays the former into a participation in the quarrels and wars of the latter without adequate inducement or justification. It leads also to concessions to the favorite nation of privileges denied to others which is apt doubly to injure the nation making the concessions; by unnecessarily parting with what ought to have been retained, and by exciting jealousy, ill-will, and a disposition to retaliate, in the parties from whom equal privileges are withheld...

> As avenues to foreign influence in innumerable ways, such attachments are particularly alarming to the truly enlightened and independent patriot. How many opportunities do they afford to tamper with domestic factions, to practice the arts of seduction, to mislead public opinion, to influence or awe the public councils. Such an attachment of a small or weak towards a great and powerful nation dooms the former to be the satellite of the latter.

> **Against the insidious wiles of foreign influence** (I conjure you to believe me, fellow-citizens) the jealousy of a free people ought to be constantly awake, since history and experience prove that foreign influence is one of the most baneful foes of republican government. But that jealousy to be useful must be impartial; else it becomes the instrument of the very influence to be avoided, instead of a defense against it. Excessive partiality for one foreign nation and excessive dislike of another cause those whom they actuate to see danger only on one side, and serve to veil and even second the arts of influence on the other. Real patriots who may resist the intrigues of the favorite are liable to become suspected and odious, while its tools and dupes usurp the applause and confidence of the people, to surrender their interests.

> The great rule of conduct for us in regard to foreign nations is in extending our commercial relations, to have with them as little

political connection as possible. So far as we have already formed engagements, let them be fulfilled with perfect good faith. Here let us stop. Europe has a set of primary interests which to us have none; or a very remote relation. Hence she must be engaged in frequent controversies, the causes of which are essentially foreign to our concerns. Hence, therefore, it must be unwise in us to implicate ourselves by artificial ties in the ordinary vicissitudes of her politics, or the ordinary combinations and collisions of her friendships or enmities.[82] (*Washington's Farewell Address*, 1796; emphasis added)

George Washington, by Charles Willson Peale, 1776[83]

---

[82] http://avalon.law.yale.edu/18th_century/washing.asp
[83] Public domain. The White House Historical Association.

"Mad" Anthony Wayne

Date	Events
January 1, 1745	Born in Easttown Township, Pennsylvania (near Paoli)
1765	Attends College of Philadelphia (now the University of Pennsylvania)
1766	• Does surveying work for Benjamin Franklin on some land owned by Franklin in Nova Scotia • Marries Mary Penrose; they would have 2 children
1767	Works in his father's tannery and as a surveyor
1775	Colonel, Continental Army
1775/76	Raises a militia unit and becomes Colonel of the 4th Pennsylvania Regiment
June 8, 1776	Participates in the Battle of Trois-Rivieres (British victory) in Quebec during Benedict Arnold's unsuccessful invasion of Canada; he would go on to lead troops at Fort Ticonderoga and Mount Independence
February 21, 1777	Promoted to Brigadier General, Continental Army
September 11, 1777	Protects the right flank of the Continental Army at the Battle of Brandywine
September 20/21, 1777	Wayne's forces are attacked at night by British forces in the Battle of Paoli. Britain wins the battle amid charges from the Continentals that the British "took no prisoners".
October 4, 1777	British victory at the Battle of Germantown, where Wayne's forces charged ahead of the Continental Army's lines, and were almost surrounded
December 19, 1777 - June 19, 1778	Winter encampment at Valley Forge
June 28, 1778	The Continental Army drives the British from the field in the Battle of Monmouth. Wayne delivers the *coup de grâce*.
July 1779	Washington assigns Wayne to head a new Corps of Light Infantry

Date	Events
July 16, 1779	At the Battle of Stony Point, New York, Wayne uses a night-time bayonet attack to rout the British. He would win a medal from the Continental Congress for his victory.
July 20/21 1780	At the Battle of Bull's Ferry, New Jersey, Wayne is defeated by the British
July 6, 1781	Wayne successfully leads an advance force under Marquis de Lafayette in a bayonet charge in the Battle of Green Spring (James City County, Virginia), a British victory
January 1, 1781	Wayne helps quell the Pennsylvania Line Mutiny by replacing parts of the Line
October 10, 1783	Promoted to Major General
1784	Serves in the Pennsylvania State legislature
1785	Moves to Georgia, and is rewarded by the State of Georgia with a tract of land in honor of his military service (Wayne had negotiated with the Creek and Cherokee Indians in Georgia at the end of the Revolutionary War)
March 4 1791 – March 24, 1792	Congressman from Georgia, but loses his seat after a House committee decides that he hadn't met the residency requirements
1792/96	Back in the saddle as a Major General
1793	• Wayne is assigned command of the *Legion of the United States* by Washington in the Northwest Indian (Shawnees and Miamis) War (which had not gone well prior to Wayne's assignment) • General Wayne Inn in Merion, Pennsylvania is renamed to honor the general
August 20, 1794	Wayne essentially ends the war with a victory at the Battle of Fallen Timbers near Maumee, Ohio. The Indian tribes were forced to sign a peace treaty, the Treaty of Greenville.
October 21, 1794	Wayne oversees the construction of Fort Wayne (Indiana)
August 3, 1795	Treaty of Greenville is signed, assigning the United States most of Ohio
December 15,	Dies at age 51 of gout, and is buried in Fort Presque

174

Date	Events
1796	Isle (Erie, Pennsylvania)
1796	Waynesburg, Pennsylvania (located in the extreme southwestern part of the state) is founded
December 7, 1803	Wayne County, Georgia is established
1809	Wayne is re-interred in Radnor, Pennsylvania
1831	Waynesboro, Pennsylvania is incorporated, and renamed in honor of Anthony Wayne
1842/51	Fort Wayne (in Detroit) is built
1883	Waynesboro (formerly Waynesborough), Georgia is incorporated
September 14, 1929	United States Post Office issues a commemorative stamp (2 cents) honoring the victory at Fallen Timbers
1939	Bruce Wayne of *Batman* fame is so named in honor of Anthony Wayne (and Robert the Bruce)
December 1992	Wayne National Forest in Ohio is established

While perhaps not the greatest Continental general, "Mad" Anthony Wayne (b. 1745; d. 1796) certainly had the best sobriquet (although Francis "Swamp Fox" Marion is in the running). Legendary for his bravery in battle, Wayne was a key part of Continental Army victories at the Battle of Stony Point (for which he was recognized by Congress) and the Battle of Green Spring (James City County, Virginia). He also protected the right flank of the Continental Army at the Battle of Brandywine on September 11, 1777.

"General Anthony Wayne", 1878[84]

Wayne's best known defeat occurred at the Battle of Paoli on September 20/21, 1777, when his forces were attacked at night. Britain won the battle amid charges from the Continentals that the British "took no prisoners". Wayne learned from the defeat, and turned the tables on the British on July 16, 1779 at the Battle of Stony Point, New York, when Wayne used a night-time bayonet attack to rout the British.

By the end of the war, Wayne had been promoted to Major-General, a title he would be given again by President Washington in 1793, when he was assigned command of the *Legion of the United States* in the Northwest Indian (Shawnees

---

[84] Library of Congress http://www.loc.gov/pictures/item/2003671510/

and Miamis) War (which had not gone well prior to Wayne's assignment). On August 20, 1794, Wayne essentially ended the war with a victory at the Battle of Fallen Timbers near Maumee, Ohio. The Indian tribes were forced to sign a peace treaty, the Treaty of Greenville.

Heroines of the American Revolution

Abigail Adams

Date	Events
November 22, 1744	Born in Weymouth, Massachusetts
October 25, 1764	Marries lawyer (and third-cousin) John Adams
1767	John Quincy Adams is born
1768	John and Abigail move to Boston
1776	"Remember the ladies" letter to John Adams and the Continental Congress
1778	John accepts a diplomatic post in France
1784	Visits her husband in Paris, where he is stationed as a diplomat
1785	Her husband becomes the first U.S. minister to the Court of St James, and Abigail accompanies him
1788	Abigail and John return home to Massachusetts (Quincy)
May 16, 1789 – March 4, 1797	Wife of the Vice-President of the United States
March 4, 1797 – March 4, 1801	First Lady of the United States
July 1798	Becomes deathly ill with "bilious fever"; she also suffered from rheumatism by this time
1800	First First Lady to occupy the White House
October 28, 1818	Dies in Quincy, Massachusetts of typhoid fever
1825/29	President John Quincy Adams
1969	Musical **1776** features letters written by Abigail Adams
June 19, 2007	Commemorative coin featuring Abigail Adams is released, under the First Spouse Program
March 2008	*John Adams* miniseries debuts on HBO, with Laura Linney portraying Abigail Adams

Abigail Adams was the second First Lady of the United States, and the first to live in the White House. She was so well-known as being an adviser to the president (John Adams), that people often referred to her as "Mrs. President". She was the first Second Lady of the United States, when her husband was vice-president under George Washington.

"First Spouse Program coin for Abigail Adams"[85]

She and her husband were separated, sometimes for months, other times for years because of his political and diplomatic responsibilities. As a result, the two wrote hundreds of letters to each other, probably at least 1200. She also maintained a sporadic correspondence with Thomas Jefferson, as well as other luminaries of the period. Although not formerly schooled, she was a voracious reader, and was well acquainted with the issues of the day. She was well-known for her support of women's rights, and her opposition to slavery.

---

[85] US Mint Pressroom Image Library, Public domain.

Perhaps her most famous letter was one she wrote to John Adams in March 31, 1776, when Adams was in Philadelphia. It is a strong statement in favor of women's rights:

> ...I desire you would Remember the Ladies, and be more generous and favourable to them than your ancestors. Do not put such unlimited power into the hands of the Husbands. Remember all Men would be tyrants if they could. If particular care and attention is not paid to the Ladies we are determined to foment a Rebellion, and will not hold ourselves bound by any Laws in which we have no voice, or Representation.
>
> That your Sex are Naturally Tyrannical is a Truth so thoroughly established as to admit of no dispute, but such of you as wish to be happy willingly give up the harsh title of Master for the more tender and endearing one of Friend. Why then, not put it out of the power of the vicious and the Lawless to use us with cruelty and indignity with impunity. Men of Sense in all Ages abhor those customs which treat us only as the vassals of your Sex. Regard us then as Beings placed by providence under your protection and in imitation of the Supreme Being make use of that power only for our happiness.[86]

John Adams' response to her letter (April 14, 1776) is also extraordinary:

> We have been told that our struggle has loosened the bonds of government everywhere; that children and apprentices were disobedient; that schools and colleges were grown turbulent; that Indians slighted their guardians, and negroes grew insolent to their masters.
>
> But your letter was the first intimation that another tribe, more numerous and powerful than all the rest, were grown discontented.
>
> This is rather too coarse a compliment, but you are so saucy, I won't blot it out.

---

[86] *Letters of Mrs. Adams: The Wife of John Adams*, by Abigail Adams, John Quincy Adams, Charles Francis Adams (Wilkins, Carter and Co., 1848)

Depend upon it, we know better than to repeal our masculine systems. Although they are in full force, you know they are little more than theory. We dare not exert our power in its full latitude. We are obliged to go fair and softly, and, in practice, you know we are the subjects.

We have only the name of masters, and rather than give up this, which would completely subject us to the despotism of the petticoat, I hope General Washington and all our brave heroes would fight.[87]

She spoke up for the education of women in this letter to John Adams dated August 14, 1776. Abigail herself had not had the benefit of schooling, although her mother had taught her to read and write:

If you complain of neglect of Education in sons, what shall I say with regard to daughters, who every day experience the want of it? With regard to the Education of my own children, I find myself soon out of my depth, destitute and deficient in every part of Education.

I most sincerely wish that some more liberal plan might be laid and executed for the Benefit of the rising Generation, and that our new Constitution may be distinguished for encouraging Learning and Virtue. If we mean to have Heroes, Statesmen and Philosophers, we should have learned women. The world perhaps would laugh at me and accuse me of vanity, But you I know have a mind too enlarged and liberal to disregard the Sentiment. If much depends as is allowed upon the early education of youth and the first principles which are instill'd take the deepest root, great benefit must arise from literary accomplishments in women.[88]

Abigail was also a devout foe of slavery, as is shown in this excerpt from a letter to John Adams dated September 24, 1774:

---

[87] *Letters of Mrs. Adams: The Wife of John Adams*, by Abigail Adams, John Quincy Adams, Charles Francis Adams (Wilkins, Carter and Co., 1848)

[88] *Letters of Mrs. Adams: The Wife of John Adams*, by Abigail Adams, John Quincy Adams, Charles Francis Adams (Wilkins, Carter and Co., 1848)

I wish most sincerely there was not a slave in this province. It always appeared a most iniquitous scheme to me — to fight ourselves for what we are daily robbing and plundering from those who have as good a right to freedom as we have.[89]

She had dim views about people who worked against her husband, especially when he was president. The following is from a letter to John Adams dated January 9, 1797, in which she expresses her opinion about Alexander Hamilton:

Hamilton I know to be a proud Spirited, conceited, aspiring Mortal always pretending to Morality, with as debauched Morals as old Franklin who is more his Model than any one I know. As great an Hypocrite as any in the U.S.

His Intrigues in the Election I despise. That he has Talents I admit but I dread none of them. I shall take no notice of his Puppy head but retain the same Opinion of him I always had and maintain the same Conduct towards him I always did, that is keep him at a distance.[90]

Abigail Adams spent time in both England and France during her husband's diplomatic tours. In the following letter (to Mrs. Warren), she compares and contrasts London and Paris, England and France:

In London the streets are also full of people, but their dress, their gait, every appearance indicates business, except on Sundays, when every person devotes the day, either at church or in walking, as is most agreeable to his fancy. But here, from the gaiety of the dress and the places they frequent, I judge pleasure is the business of life. We have no days with us, or rather in our country, by which I can give you an idea of the Sabbath here, except commencement and election. Paris upon that day pours forth all her citizens into the environs for the purposes of

[89] *Letters of Mrs. Adams: The Wife of John Adams*, by Abigail Adams, John Quincy Adams, Charles Francis Adams (Wilkins, Carter and Co., 1848)
[90] *Letters of Mrs. Adams: The Wife of John Adams*, by Abigail Adams, John Quincy Adams, Charles Francis Adams (Wilkins, Carter and Co., 1848)

recreation. We have a beautiful wood cut into walks within a few rods [5.5 yards] of our dwelling, which, upon this day, resounds with music and dancing, jollity and mirth of every kind. In this wood booths are erected, where cake, fruit, and wine are sold. Here milliners repair with their gauzes, ribbons, and many other articles, in the peddling style, but for other purposes I imagine than the mere sale of their merchandise. But every thing here is a subject of merchandise.

I believe this nation is the only one in the world which could make pleasure the business of life; and yet retain such a relish for it as never to complain of its being tasteless or insipid; the Parisians seem to have exhausted nature and art in this science, and to be "triste" ["sad"] is a complaint of a most serious nature...Which of the two countries can you form the most favorable opinion of, and which is the least pernicious to the morals? That where vice is licensed; or where it is suffered to walk at large, soliciting the unwary and unguarded, as it is to a most astonishing height in the streets of London, and where virtuous females are frequently subject to insults. In Paris no such thing happens; but the greatest decency and respect is shown by all orders to the female character. The stage is in London made use of as a vehicle to corrupt the morals. In Paris no such thing is permitted. They are too polite to wound the ear. In one country vice is like a ferocious beast, seeking whom it may devour; in the other like a subtle poison, secretly penetrating and working destruction. In one country, you cannot travel a mile without danger to your person and property, yet public executions abound; in the other, your person and property are safe; executions are very rare, but in a lawful way, beware; for with whomsoever you have to deal, you may rely upon an attempt to overreach you...

Decency and good order are preserved [in France], yet are they equally crowded with those of London; but in London, at going in and coming out of the theatre, you find yourself in a mob, and are every moment in danger of being robbed. In short, the term John Bull, which Swift formerly gave to the English nation, is still very applicable to their manners. The cleanliness of Britain, joined to the civility and politeness of France, could make a most agreeable assemblage. You will smile at my choice, but as I am likely to reside some time in this country, why should I not wish them the article in which they are most deficient?[91] (Letter to Mrs. Warren, September 5, 1784)

Finally, a description of the unfinished White House is well worth reading. This comes from a letter to her daughter, dated November 21, 1800:

I ARRIVED here on Sunday last, and without meeting with any accident worth noticing, except losing ourselves when we left Baltimore, and going eight or nine miles on the Frederick road, by which means we were obliged to go the other eight through woods, where we wandered two hours without finding a guide, or the path. Fortunately, a straggling black came up with us, and we engaged him as a guide, to extricate us out of our difficulty; but woods are all you see, from Baltimore until you reach the city...

In the city there are buildings enough, if they were compact and finished, to accommodate Congress and those attached to it; but as they are, and scattered as they are, I see no great comfort for them. The river, which runs up to Alexandria, is in full view of my window, and I see the vessels as they pass and repass. The house is upon a grand and superb scale, requiring about thirty servants to attend and keep the apartments in proper order, and perform the ordinary business of the house and stables; an establishment very well proportioned to the President's salary. The lighting the apartments, from the kitchen to parlors and chambers, is a tax indeed; and the fires we are obliged to keep to secure us from daily agues is another very cheering comfort. To assist us in this great castle, and render less attendance necessary, bells are wholly wanting, not one single one being hung through the whole house, and promises are all you can obtain. This is so great an inconvenience, that I know not what to do, or how to do...if they will put me up some bells, and let me have wood enough to keep fires, I design to be pleased. I could content myself almost anywhere three months; but, surrounded with forests, can you believe that wood is not to be had, because people cannot be found to cut and cart it!...We have, indeed, come into a new country.

---

[91] *Letters of Mrs. Adams: The Wife of John Adams*, by Abigail Adams, John Quincy Adams, Charles Francis Adams (Wilkins, Carter and Co., 1848)

You must keep all this to yourself, and, when asked how I like it, say that I write you the situation is beautiful, which is true. The house is made habitable, but there is not a single apartment finished, and all withinside, except the plastering, has been done since Briesler came. We have not the least fence, yard, or other convenience, without, and the great unfinished audience-room I make a drying room of, to hang up the clothes in. The principal stairs are not up, and will not be this winter. Six chambers are made comfortable; two are occupied by the President and Mr. Shaw; two lower rooms, one for a common parlor, and one for a levee-room. Up stairs there is the oval room, which is designed for the drawing-room, and has the crimson furniture in it. It is a very handsome room now; but, when completed, it will be beautiful. If the twelve years, in which this place has been considered as the future seat of government, had been improved, as they would have been if in New England, very many of the present inconveniences would have been removed. It is a beautiful spot, capable of every improvement, and, the more I view it, the more I am delighted with it.[92]

---

[92] *Letters of Mrs. Adams: The Wife of John Adams*, by Abigail Adams, John Quincy Adams, Charles Francis Adams (Wilkins, Carter and Co., 1848)

Margaret Cochran Corbin

Date	Events
November 12, 1751	Born near Chambersburg, Pennsylvania (other sources say she was born in Ireland)
1756	Margaret's father is killed and her mother kidnapped during an Indian Raid
1758	There is a report that Margaret's mother was seen in Ohio
1772	Marries John Corbin
1775	John joins the militia (possibly the First Company of the Pennsylvania Artillery), and Margaret comes with him as a "camp follower" - cooking, cleaning, laundry
November 16, 1776	Battle of Fort Washington in Manhattan; Margaret takes over firing the cannon after both her husband and the other male member of the crew is killed. Margaret is severely wounded. She is captured by the British and later paroled.
June 26, 1777	Granted $30.00 by the Commonwealth of Pennsylvania for her bravery, and for her injuries
July 6, 1779	Awarded a half-pension by the Continental Congress
1782	Remarries an invalid soldier (d. 1783)
1783	Discharged from the Continental Army Invalid regiment
January 16, 1800	Dies near West Point, New York
1909	Commemorative plaque erected in New York City's Fort Tryon Park
April 14, 1926	The New York State Society of the Daughters of the American Revolution tracks down her grave - Her remains are then re-interred at West Point with full military honors
1977	The New York City Council names the road entering Fort Tyron Park (Fort Washington) Margaret Corbin Circle
1982	Commemorative plaque erected at 190th Street and Fort Washington Avenue

Margaret Corbin was born n 1751, probably in Chambersburg, Pennsylvania. She lost both her parents in an Indian raid in 1756 – her father was killed, and her mother kidnapped. Margaret was raised by an uncle.

"Was a brave Woman. Takes Her Dead Husband's Place at the Gun"[93]

In 1772, she married John Corbin, who joined the Pennsylvania militia in 1775. When he went to war, Margaret went with him as a "camp follower" - a woman who helped with the washing, cooking, laundry, etc.

Her great claim to fame came on November 16, 1776 during the battle of Fort Washington in northern Manhattan. Her husband, acting as an artillery "matross" was killed, as were the rest of the gun crew. Margaret immediately took the place of the gun crew, and kept firing the gun with deadly accuracy. She was hit three times with bullets, and also

---

[93] *Dakota Farmers' Leader,* (Canton, S.D.), July 3, 1896

suffered shrapnel injuries. Her left arm was injured to the extent that she was never able to use it again.

Margaret was captured by the British, and later was involved in a prisoner exchange. She was assigned to the Pennsylvania "Invalid Brigade", and was awarded $30 by the Commonwealth of Pennsylvania in 1777 for her bravery, and for her injuries. Later, she was awarded a half pension by the Continental Congress, the only women to receive a military pension in the Revolutionary War.

She was mustered out of the Invalid regiment in 1783. She died in 1800.

A typical example of the Margaret Corbin story is shown here:

WAS A BRAVE WOMAN
TAKES HER DEAD HUSBAND'S PLACE AT THE GUN.
When He Was Shot Margaret Corbin Faced the Foe While Scores of Men Hastened to Get Away—Ranks with the Maid of Saragossa [a Spanish heroine].

As a Cannoneer in a Battle.

Margaret Corbin, a New York woman, whose bravery ranks her with Byron's famous heroine, the maid of Saragossa, and also with the maid of Domremy [Joan D'Arc], is comparatively unknown to the world. Historians overlooked one of the grandest women that ever trod the earth, when they failed to tell of the deed of heroism done by Margaret Corbin during the battle of Port Washington. A few lines in an encyclopedia tell something of her, but no place else is there a word about her.

It was in the defense of New York city that Margaret Corbin showed herself as a courageous and brave woman. In the battle of Harlem plains—first and last of importance to be fought on the Island of Manhattan—hers was the only deed of shining valor that gave the surrender of Fort Washington the glory of victorious resistance. There were incompetence, lack of arms, pusillanimity

189

—indeed, it was there at Fort Washington that treachery like Arnold's, only more successful, was practiced. Some men died bravely. One of them Margaret Corbin's husband.

He was serving a cannon against the Hessians in one of the redoubts which stayed the advance of the enemy on the fort. Baron Kuyphausen was directing his well-disciplined troops according to the information taken through the lines by the traitor. Off to the southeast Lord Percy was pressing with superior confidence and numbers upon the earthworks defended by Col. Cadwalader of Philadelphia. Just as hope was departing, and the Americans were falling back, here and there, one gunner was rendered conspicuous by standing his ground. It was Corbin, a Pennsylvania man, and by his side his tidy little wife, cheeks flaming with exertion and excitement, labored to speed his loading and firing.

Suddenly Corbin dropped and rolled to his wife's feet, dead. The fragile woman stepped to the gun, swabbed it, rammed home the shot and touched off the charges, valiantly determined not to yield what her husband died to retain. There was only hostile faces around, and she was alone and isolated. Presently, wounded by three grapeshot, she fell. She hadn't saved the oriflame banner like Jeanne d'Arc, but she had shown again that there is one thing that woman can do as well as the best of men—they can die grandly!

It was due rather to a stanch constitution than to tender nursing that Margaret Corbin did not come to her death by those linked balls. Three years later, in 1779, the council of Pennsylvania appealed on her behalf to the board of war, and in consequence she received from Congress a pension of one-half the monthly pay of a soldier in service. Learning, in the year following, that her injuries deprived her of the use of one arm, the Government allowed her "one complete suit of clothes out of the public stores," or the value thereof in money in addition to the provision previously made. That, and the title of "patriot" in the records, which is a fine title to hold and deserve, is all the recognition which her service ever got.

It was thirty-three years afterward that the maid of Saragossa imitated Margaret Corbin's bravery, and received the renown that should have been bestowed upon the heroine of the battle at Fort Washington.[94]

It is instructive to examine the language of the government involving the payments made to her after she was invalided.

In Council
Philadelphia June 29, 1779
Ordered,
That the case of Margaret Corbin who was wounded and utterly disabled at Fort Washington **while she heroically filled the post of her husband who was killed by her side serving a piece of artillery,** be recommended to a further consideration of the Board of War. This Council being of opinion that notwithstanding the rations which have been allowed her, she is not provided for as her helpless situation really requires

Extract from the minutes
T. Matlack, Sec'y
Note. The Council have given her thirty dollars to relieve her present necessities, until her case can be provided for in a more effectual manner.
Hnble Board of War[95]

War Office 3d July, 1779
The inclosed recommendation of the Council of Pennsylvania in favour of Margaret Corbin, added to many circumstances which appear to support her petition for relief, induce the board to offer a resolution, which they think her peculiar situation merits.— **As she had fortitude and virtue enough to supply the place of her husband after his fall in the service of his country, and in the execution of that task received the dangerous wound under which she now labors, the board can but consider her as entitled to the same grateful return which would be made to a soldier in circumstances equally unfortunate**: They therefore beg leave to report:

---

[94] *Dakota Farmers' Leader,* (Canton, S.D.), July 3, 1896
[95] *The Magazine of American History with Notes and Queries, Volume 16*, by Martha Joanna Lamb (Historical Publication Company, 1886)

That Margaret Corbin, who was wounded and disabled in the attack on Fort Washington whilst she heroically filled the post of her husband who was killed by her side serving a piece of artillery; do receive during her natural life, or the continuance of such disability, the one half of the monthly pay drawn by a soldier in the service of these states: and that she now receive out of the public stores one complete suit of soldiers clothing, or the value thereof in money.

I am with the utmost respect
Your Excellencys most obed. Servant
P. Scull, Sec'y.
His Excellency John Jay, Esqure [96]

At a Board of War, July 24, 1780

Present Col. Pickering, Gen. Scott, Mr. Peters, Gen. Ward, Col. Grayson

The board having recd information that Margaret Corbin (for whom Congress made provision in their Act of July 6, 1779, for her **Gallant Conduct in serving a piece of artillery when her husband was killed by her side**) still remains in a deplorable situation in consequence of her wound, by which she is deprived of the use of one arm—and is in other respects much disabled—and probably will continue a Cripple during her Life— Beg leave to report:

That Margaret Corbin receive annually during her natural Life, one compleat suit of cloaths out of the Public Stores—or the value thereof in money in addition to the provision made for her by the Act of Congress of July 3, 1779.

Extract from the minutes
Ben. Stodert, Sec'y
His Excellency
The President of Congress.[97]

---

[96] *The Magazine of American History with Notes and Queries, Volume 16*, by Martha Joanna Lamb (Historical Publication Company, 1886)
[97] *The Magazine of American History with Notes and Queries, Volume 16*, by Martha Joanna Lamb (Historical Publication Company, 1886)

Margaret Corbin had some powerful advocates, including General Henry Knox, Secretary of War. The following excerpts are from letters sent to Henry Knox by Major George Fleming, the Commander at West Point, apprising Knox of her condition when she lived near West Point near the end of her life.

West Point, 7th of October, 1786. Sir: I have sent another account of Mrs. Swims for taking care of Captain Molly up to the 27th of September, and have removed her to another place, as I thought she was not as well treated as she ought to be.

West Point, April 21st, 1787. Sir: I am informed by the woman that takes care of Captain Molly, that she is much in want of shifts. If you think proper to order three or four, I should be very glad.

West Point, June 12th, 1787. Sir: If the shifts which you informed me should be made for Captain Molly are done, I should be glad to have them sent, as she complains much for the want of them.[98]

This may be the first and only time that a Secretary of War asked to be apprised of the situation regarding ladies shifts (loose fitting dresses).

It should be pointed out that Margaret was not a particularly dainty lady. At one point after the battles, the Philadelphia Society of Women was planning on erecting a monument in honor of her exploits. They choose not to do so after meeting her. She was rough, she drank and she smoked. And the following description indicates that he language may not have been especially dainty either.

Molly is described as usually appearing with an artillery-man's coat over her skirts. She was brusque, coarse, red-haired, wholly

[98] *General Orders of Geo. Washington: Issued at Newburgh 1782-1783*, compiled by Edward C. Boynton (E. N. Ruttenbur, 1883)

wanting in feminine charms, and one of her biographers has recorded that she made use of— swear words.[99]

There is some difficulty tracing the story of Margaret Corbin, as there is obviously confusion between her and another battlefield heroine from a year later – Molly Pitcher, at the Battle of Monmouth.   In some accounts in the 19th century, Margaret is referred to as "Captain Molly", and is even identified as carrying a pitcher of water when her husband dies.

However, there doesn't seem to be any question that Margaret Corbin really existed, or that she did what she was said to have done.

---

[99] *General Orders of Geo. Washington: Issued at Newburgh 1782-1783*, compiled by Edward C. Boynton (E. N. Ruttenbur, 1883)

Lydia Barrington Darragh

Lydia Barrington Darragh was born in Ireland c. 1728. She and her husband, William, emigrated to the United States in 1756, and settled in Philadelphia. It was in the City of Brotherly Love that Lydia made her mark on the American Revolution, acting as a spy and assisting the Colonials in winning the battle of Whitemarsh.

There are at least three accounts by contemporaries chronicling Lydia's exploits. I include the one from her daughter, Ann Darragh, below. But to summarize, when the British occupied Philadelphia in September of 1776, General Williams Howe confiscated a back room in the Darragh house to use as a conference room for his staff. Lydia was pressed into service at a number of meetings to act as hostess, and was soon accepted by the British officers. She began chronicling what was said at the meetings, and arranged for her coded messages to be sent to General Washington. In one version, it was her 14 year old son John who did the delivery of the messages.

On December 2, 1777, everything changed. Lydia was informed by Major John Andre that she and her family needed to retire to their chambers before a private evening meeting in their parlor. Lydia crept down the stairs and listened in on the meeting from a closet. What she heard was a bombshell - the British planned on attacking Washington at Whitemarsh!

The next day (December 3, 1777), under the pretext of leaving the city to get flour for her family, Lydia used a pass from the British to pass through their lines to the Rising Sun Tavern, north of Philadelphia. Just to the west of the Tavern, she passed her information to Colonel Craig, of the Light Infantry – a man she already knew. The information was passed on to

Washington, and the Colonials were prepared for Howe's offensive against them on December 5/8, 1777. The Colonials retained control of the field, and Howe retreated to Philadelphia.

Date	Events
1728	Born in Dublin, Ireland
November 2, 1753	Marries William Darragh in Dublin, Ireland
1756	Lydia and William emigrate to America, and settle in Philadelphia
September 26, 1777	British occupy Philadelphia; the Darragh home (Loxley House) on Second Street, below Spruce Street, is confiscated by the British for use as a billet for his staff, and a conference area. Lydia is told she must vacate the house.
c. September 27, 1777	After a chance meeting with her second cousin Captain William Barrington[100], he intercedes on her behalf with Howe, who removes the eviction notice, but still plans on using the Darragh house for conferences.
October through November, 1777	Serving as a hostess during the British staff meetings at her house, Lydia writes down (possibly in cipher) information she gleans, and sends it to Washington
December 2, 1777	Lydia is informed by Major John Andre that she and her family must retire to their chambers before a private evening meeting in their parlor. Lydia spies on the meeting from closet, and reports what she hears to Washington – the British will attack Washington at Whitemarsh!
December 3, 1777	Under the pretext of leaving the city to get flour for her family, Lydia receives a pass from her second cousin, and travels north of Philadelphia. Lydia passes on her information to Washington's forces.
December 5/8, 1777	Continental Army victory at Whitemarsh
April 27, 1781	Her son Charles is removed from the rolls of the

[100] Some accounts simply say that the person she met was a fellow Irishman

196

Date	Events
	Friends of Philadelphia for fighting with the Colonials
1783	Lydia is removed from the rolls of the *Friends of Philadelphia* for "neglecting to attend our religious meetings"
June 8, 1783	William Darragh dies
December 28, 1789	Dies in Philadelphia, and is buried at Fourth and Arch Streets
1827	The chronicle of Lydia smuggling information to Washington about the British plans to march on Whitemarsh first appears, in the *American Quarterly Review*
1906	The journals of General Elias Boudinot are published, in which he confirms that the information delivered by Lydia Barrington Darragh was, indeed, delivered to Washington before the attack

Below is an account of Lydia's spying career from her daughter Ann.

ANN DARRACH'S ACCOUNT

In the winter of 1777 and 1778 General Howe, commander of the British forces in Philadelphia, had his headquarters in the house of Mr. Cadwalader on Second Street, near Little Dock. The house occupied by William Darragh was nearly opposite. William Darragh was ordered to open his house for the accommodation of some of the troops and find other quarters for his family. It was a cold winter. the city was crowded and he knew not what to do, but finally Lydia determined to go herself to General Howe and ask for relief. While she was waiting for an audience one of the staff officers entered into conversation with her, and finding she was, as well as himself, a native of Ireland, became rather interested in her statement of her difficulties and asked General Howe to relieve her from the order. This he declined to do, saying they also were very much pressed for room, but at length decided to take only one room for a council chamber. This was large and at the back of the house. This quieted Lydia very much, for she had a son, her eldest, a lieutenant in General Washington's army, then at White Marsh, and all her sympathies were with these poorly clad and half-starved patriots, and to have her house used as a place in which to lay plans for their destruction was a bitter trial. She was, for want of room, obliged to send her younger children to the country home of a relative of her husband.

Councils were frequently held in the upper chamber, much to the distress of the mistress of the house. One day (Tuesday, December 2d) an officer came and told her to have all her family in bed at an early hour, as they wished to use the room that night free from interruption. She promised to do so, and when all was quiet lay down herself, but could not sleep. A presentiment of evil weighed down her spirits, and at last, hearing loud talking, went into a closet, separated from the council room by a thin board partition covered with paper, just in time to hear the reading of the minutes of the council, then concluding. The orders were: 'The troops should march out on a certain night (Robert Walsh, "late in the evening of the 4th"), attack Washington's army, and with their superior force and the unprepared condition of the enemy victory was certain.' A sharp pang shot through her heart. Patriotic she was, but perhaps motherly love had a large share in forming a resolution to do something to save the army of which her son was a member. She returned to bed, and when an officer knocked to waken her to fasten up the house after their departure she did not answer until the third summons. The next day (Wednesday, December3d) was spent in planning some mode of action. That night she told her husband she was going to use a pass she had obtained some time before to go to the country to see her children (Robert Walsh states she was going to the Frankford mill for flour), and, starting early the next morning (Thursday, December 4th). and going in the direction named in her pass (Robert Walsh states she left her bag at the Frankford mill), but soon changing her course, after a long and weary walk, came near the American camp. She saw an officer approaching on horseback. It proved to be Colonel Craig, of the Light Infantry, whom she knew. He was greatly surprised to see her, and asked, 'Why, Mrs. Darragh, what are you doing so far from home?' She asked him to walk beside her, which he did, leading his horse. In low tones she told him the important intelligence she had risked so much to bring, and he at once rode with it to headquarters. (Robert Walsh states that before Craig left Lydia he took her to a house near at hand and directed a female in it to give her something to eat.) Lydia then returned home, but did not tell her husband the real

198

object of her errand to the country until she thought all danger over.

He little knew the part his wife had played in the drama of that eventful night. She feared the least suspicion of his having taken information out of the city might endanger his life and kept her secret. That night she sat at a front window, wrapped in a cloak, and watched the soldiery march by on their way to attack Washington. The next day was spent in an agony of fear, for even when the troops returned she was uncertain what the result was. There were many rumors, but she did not dare to ask a question.

When nearly dusk an officer came to the house, called her to the council room, and then locked the door. She was so faint she would have fallen if he had not handed her a chair and asked her to be seated. The room was nearly dark, and he could not see the pallor of her face. Then he inquired if any of her family were awake on the night of their last council. She replied: 'No, they were all in bed and asleep.' Then he said: 'I need not ask you, for we had great difficulty in waking you to fasten the door after us. But one thing is certain; the enemy had notice of our coming, were prepared for us, and we marched back like a parcel of damned fools. The walls must have some ears.' She retained her possession through all the interview. 'I never told a lie about it,' she would say, 'I could answer all his questions without that.'

The dear old narrator of these events, herself a strict Quakeress, would always add: "Ah! if my dear mother could only see the pictures of herself in the children's histories, flounced and furbelowed[101], how shocked she would be."[102]

---

[101] A ruffle in a dress or skirt

[102] *Lydia Darragh, One of the Heroines of the Revolution*, by Henry Darrach (City History Society of Philadelphia, 1916)

Nancy Hart

Nancy Morgan Hart, born c. 1735 in North Carolina[103] was the primary heroine of the American Revolution in Georgia. She served as a Colonial spy, a harborer of Colonial fugitives, and, in one instance, judge, jury and executioner of a group of British marauders.

"Nancy Hart, a heroine of the Revolution"[104]

Nancy was known to be a bit hot-headed and domineering, and there are many stories about her temper, as this one anecdote shows:

> Nancy Hart's maiden name was Morgan. She was married to Benjamin Hart, and soon afterwards came to Georgia...
>
> Among the anecdotes remembered by Mr. Snead is the following: On one evening she was at home with her children, sitting round the log-fire, with a large pot of soap boiling over the fire. Nancy was busy stirring the soap, and entertaining her family with the latest news of the war.

---

[103] Some sources say she was born in Pennsylvania
[104] Library of Congress http://www.loc.gov/pictures/item/2012645953/

The houses in those days were all built of logs, as well as the chimneys. 'While they were thus employed, one of the family discovered some one from the outside peeping through the crevices of the chimney, and gave a silent intimation of it to Nancy. She rattled away with more and more spirit, now giving exaggerated accounts of the discomfiture of the Tories, and again stirring the boiling soap, and watching the place indicated for a re-appearance of the spy. Suddenly, with the quickness of lightning, she dashed the ladle of boiling soap through the crevice full in the face of the eavesdropper, who, taken by surprise, and blinded by the hot soap, screamed and roared at a tremendous rate, whilst the indomitable Nancy went out, amused herself at his expense, and, with gibes and taunts, bound him fast as her prisoner...[105]

Date	Events
c. 1735	Born in North Carolina. Nancy was the cousin of General Daniel Morgan.
c. 1771	Hart family moves to northeastern Georgia
Revolutionary War	Hart kills several British soldiers who have demanded that she feed them
1780s	Harts briefly move to Brunswick, Georgia, where Benjamin Hart dies
1803	Nancy son, John Hart, moves the family to Henderson County, Kentucky
1830	Dies in Henderson County, Kentucky
December 7, 1853	Hart County Georgia is founded, named after Nancy Hart
June 1861	The Nancy Harts, an all-female military company is formed in LaGrange, Georgia. It was the Nancy Harts that surrendered LaGrange to Colonel Oscar Hugh La Grange on April 17, 1865.
October 5, 1900	The Nancy Hart Chapter, National Society of the Daughters of the American Revolution (NSDAR) in Milledgeville, Georgia is formed
1912	Workers on the Elberton and Eastern Railroad near the location of the old Hart cabin discover five or six skeletons buried in a row with their necks snapped
1930s	Civilian Conservation Corps builds a replica cabin on the site of the original Hart cabin in Elbert County, Georgia

---

[105] *The Romance of the Revolution*, by Oliver Bell Bunce (Porter & Coates, 1870)

Date	Events
1950	Lake Hartwell is named for Nancy Hart
1997	Hart is inducted into the GWA (Georgia Women of Achievement)

Our Pioneer Mothers

with being one of the best shots on the Broad and her cabin walls were hung with antlers and other spoils of the chase of her own bringing in. Her instinct in the location of a "bee tree" was as unerring as it was valuable in a new country where sweets were scarce and hard to get. And always she was on the lookout for plants and herbs the curative properties of which she was credited with knowing more about than any other person in the section. Indeed her skill as a doctor was called upon from far and near. Her skill and knowledge seem also to have taken a wider scope, as it is recorded that she held a tract of land by the safe tenure of a first survey which she had made herself, hatchet in hand.

Though not in the path of the war and its devastations, the Harts were made to feel its blighting breath. The sympathizers with the British cause in that section of the country were numerous, powerful and of most pernicious activity. It was a sparsely settled community. All the lazy, lawless, cattle-stealing element took advantage of the times to ally itself with the Tories as a cloak for its own depreciations, and the chance it gave to pay off old grudges. Many of the Whigs, as the patriots were called, were driven to take refuge in the swamps and cane-country, shooting and hanging the Whigs wherever they could be found and stealing or wantonly destroying their property.

Benjamin Hart was a man of some means, and frequently found it necessary to gather up his stock and slaves and disappear in the canebrakes, in the fastnesses of which the Tories dared not follow. He was better off than many of the others, as he rested secure in the belief that the resourceful wife was competent to take care of herself and family. Indeed, it has been inti-

mated that the good man sometimes welcomed these enforced periods of retirement, as it gave him relief from the scolding of his domineering and not too amiable spouse.

It was during one of these enforced absences of the many heads of families

out and tell your father that I've got six d—n Tories, an' he'd better come an' get 'em." Nancy Hart was said to be somewhat cross-eyed, and it may be that each man at the table believed that rifle to be aimed directly at him. Anyway none of them moved. The

"I'LL BLOW THE HEAD OFF THE MAN WHO TRIES TO EAT."

in that section that the Tories determined upon breaking into the fast-

Tories were allowed to finish their dinner and were then taken in charge by the Whigs. Nancy Hart gained con-

"Our Pioneer Mothers"[106]

Nancy achieved her everlasting fame because of an encounter she had with several British soldiers in her cabin in Elberton County, Georgia. Details differ in different tellings of the tale, but here are some of the basics (alternative details in parenthesis).

- A group of five (or six) British marauders showed up at the Hart farm in Georgia. They had just come from killing a Colonial colonel. They were looking for an escaped Colonial spy which Nancy Hart had, indeed, aided (or they were just there to get something to eat).

---

[106] *Salt Lake Tribune*, August 21, 1910

- The soldiers forced themselves inside the cabin, and demanded the Nancy fix them a meal (the soldiers may have killed the sole turkey owned by the Hart family). The soldiers stacked their guns in the corner of the cabin.
- Nancy prepared a meal, and made sure the soldiers had plenty of wine. Once the were a bit drunk, she passed their guns out through a hole in the cabin wall to here daughter, keeping one for herself.
- Nancy told he daughter to sound the alarm using a conch shell that was outside the cabin on a stump.
- Nancy pointed a rifle at the soldiers, and told them not to move. When one soldier made a move towards where the rifles had been stacked, Nancy shot him dead. Some sources indicated that the soldiers couldn't tell where Nancy was looking because she was cross-eyed (other sources say she wasn't cross-eyed).
- Responding to the conch alarm, Nancy's husband Benjamin, and perhaps some other men arrived at the cabin. They wanted to shoot the rest of the soldiers, but Nancy demanded that they be hung instead.
- The soldiers were hung.

Below is an early account of the encounter, from a 1870 book:

The following, from Mrs. Ellet's "Women of the Revolution," will be read with interest...

In this county is a stream, formerly known as "War-woman's Creek." Its name was derived from the character of an individual who lived near the entrance of the stream into the river. This person was Nancy Hart, a woman ignorant of letters and the civilities of life, but a zealous lover of liberty and the "liberty boys," as she called the Whigs. She had a husband, whom she denominated "a poor stick," because he did not take a decided and active part with the defenders of his country, although she could not conscientiously charge him with the least partiality towards the Tories. This vulgar and illiterate, but hospitable and valorous female patriot, could boast no share of beauty—a fact she herself would have readily acknowledged, had she ever enjoyed an opportunity of looking in a mirror. She was crosseyed, with a broad, angular mouth, ungainly in figure, rude in speech, and awkward in manners, but having a woman's heart for her friends, though that of a Catrine Montour [possibly, a noted Iroquois woman in the late 1700s] for the enemies of her country. She was well known to the Tories, who stood in fear of her revenge for any grievance or aggressive act, though they let pass no opportunity of worrying and annoying her, when they could do so with impunity.

On the occasion of an excursion from the British camp at Augusta, a party of Tories penetrated into the interior, and having savagely murdered Colonel Dooly in bed, in his own house, they proceeded up the country for the purpose of perpetrating further atrocities. On their way, a detachment of five of the party diverged to the east, and crossed Broad River, to make discoveries about the neighborhood, and pay a visit to their old acquaintance, Nancy Hart. On reaching her cabin, they entered it unceremoniously, receiving from her no welcome but a scowl, and informed her they had come to know the truth of a story current respecting her, that she had secreted a noted rebel from a company of King's men who were pursuing him, and who, but for her aid, would have caught and hung him. Nancy undauntedly avowed her agency in the fugitive's escape...

[They ordered] her to aid and comfort them by giving them something to eat. She replied, "I never feed King's men, if I can help it. The villains have put it out of my power to feed even my own family and friends, by stealing and killing all my poultry and pigs, except that one old gobbler you see in the yard."

"'Well, and that you shall cook for us," said one, who appeared the head of the party; and raising his musket, he shot down the turkey, which another of the men brought into the house, and handed to Mrs. Hart, to clean and cook without delay. She stormed and swore awhile—for Nancy occasionally swore—but seeming, at last, resolved to make a merit of necessity, began with alacrity the arrangements for cooking, assisted by her daughter, a little girl some ten or twelve years old, and sometimes by one of the soldiers, with whom she seemed in a tolerably good humor, exchanging rude jests with him. The Tories, pleased with her freedom, invited her to partake of the liquor they had brought with them, an invitation which was accepted with witty thanks.

The spring, of which every settlement has one near at hand, was just at the edge of the swamp, and a short distance within it was a high snag-topped stump, on which was placed a conch shell. This rude trumpet was used by the family to give information, by means of a variation of notes, to Mr. Hart, or his neighbors, who might be at work in the field or clearing just beyond the swamp, that the "Britishers" or Tories were about, that the master was wanted at the cabin, or that he was to "keep close," or "make tracks" for another swamp. Pending the operations of cooking, Mrs. Hart had sent her daughter, Sukey, to the spring for water, with directions to blow the conch in such a way as would inform him that there were Tories in the cabin, and that he should "keep close," with his three neighbors who were with him, till he heard the conch again.

The party had become merry over their jug, and sat down to feast upon the slaughtered gobbler. They had cautiously stacked their arms where they were in view, and within reach; and Mrs. Hart, assiduous in her attentions upon the table and to her guests, occasionally passed between them and their muskets. Water was called for, and as there was none in the cabin—Mrs. Hart having so contrived that—Sukey was again sent to the spring, instructed by her mother to blow the conch so as to call up Mr. Hart and his neighbors immediately. Meanwhile, Mrs. Hart had slipped out one of the pieces of pine which constitutes a "chinking" between the logs of a cabin, and had dexterously put out of the house, through that space, two of the five guns. She was detected in the act of putting out the third. The party sprang to their feet. Quick as thought, Mrs. Hart brought the piece she held to her shoulder, and declared she would kill the first man who approached her. All were terror-struck, for Nancy's obliquity of sight caused each one to imagine her aim was at him. At length one of them made a motion to advance upon her. True to her threat, she fired. He fell dead upon the floor! Instantly seizing another musket, she brought it to the position in readiness to fire again. By this time Sukey had returned from the spring, and taking up the remaining gun, carried it out of the house, saying to her mother, "Daddy and them will soon be here." This information increased the alarm of the Tories, who understood the necessity of recovering their arms

205

immediately. But each hesitated, in the confident belief that Mrs. Hart had one eye, at least, upon him for a mark. They proposed a general rush. No time was to be lost by the bold woman; she fired again, and brought down another Tory. Sukey had another musket in readiness, which her mother took, and, posting herself in the doorway, called upon the party to "surrender their d____d Tory carcasses to a Whig woman."

They agreed to surrender, and proposed to "shake hands upon the strength of it;" but the conqueror kept them in their places for a few moments, till her husband and his neighbors came up to the door. They were about to shoot down the Tories, but Mrs. Hart stopped them, saying they had surrendered to her, and, her spirit being up to boiling heat, she swore that " shooting was too good for them." This hint was enough. The dead man was dragged out of the house, the wounded Tory and the others were bound, taken out beyond the bars, and hung. The tree upon which they were hung was pointed out, in 1838, by one who lived in those bloody times, and who also showed the spot once occupied by Mrs. Hart's cabin, accompanying the designation with the emphatic remark, "Poor Nancy—she was a honey of a patriot, but the devil of a wife."[107]

It is said that later in her life, Nancy went through a religious conversion, and started attending camp meetings. She approached her duties as a new convert with the same gusto to which she approached her duty as a Colonial spy.

Tradition says that Nancy Hart was converted at one of these [camp] meetings. It would be reasonable to suppose that time and hardships would have touched the red hair with gray and curbed the old dauntless spirit, but she was as strenuous in religion as in politics. There are mystical stories In my mind of a gaunt old woman embracing my dignified ancestor and disarranging his stock and dragging sluggard sinners by their queues and coat tails to the penance seat, but these are traditions repeated from generation to generation and I would not vouch for their authenticity.[108]

---

[107] *The Romance of the Revolution*, by Oliver Bell Bunce (Porter & Coates, 1870)
[108] *Perrysburg Journal*, (Perrysburg, Wood Co., O. [Ohio]), March 16, 1906

In 1853, Hart County, Georgia was named in her honor, and, a 100 years later, Lake Hartwell was also named in her honor. During the Civil War, a group of women in LaGrange, Georgia formed the *Nancy Harts*, a militia company which conducted drills throughout the war. It was the *Nancy Harts* which surrendered LaGrange to Colonel Oscar Hugh La Grange on April 17, 1865 (the day after Columbus and West Point had fallen).

Lucy Flucker Knox

Lucy Knox was born in 1756, the daughter of Thomas Flucker, the Royal Secretary of the Province of Massachusetts. She fell in love with bookseller Henry Knox around 1773, and married him in 1774 over the objections of her family. The family objected both on issues of class (Knox was born poor) and politics (Henry leaned towards the Colonial side).

In 1775, after the Battles of Lexington and Concord, Lucy and Henry fled Boston, and Henry's business was trashed by the British. Throughout the rest of the Revolutionary War, Lucy and her husband had no fixed address. Her family in Boston returned to England after the British evacuated Boston in March 1776.

Out of loyalty to her husband, Lucy spent as much time with her husband during the War as possible. She is famous for her time at Valley Forge when she, along with Martha Washington, sewed and mended clothing for the troops, and attended to the ill.

After the War, Henry became Secretary of War, a position he held from 1785/95. In 1795, Lucy and Henry retired to Montpelier in Thomaston, Maine. Lucy had inherited all of her families properties that were abandoned when they had returned to England in March 1776.

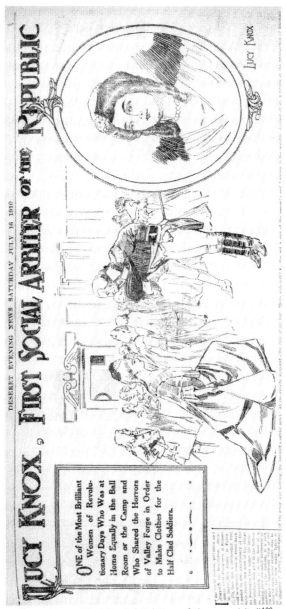

"Lucy Knox: First Social Arbiter of the republic"[109]

The following is a description of Lucy Knox and her role in the Revolution from an 1818 book.

---

[109] *Deseret Evening News,* (Deseret, Utah) July 16, 1910

In various journals we find the presence of Mrs. Knox noticed in camp. Chastellux describes the hut on a small farm where she lived with her children, a short distance from head-quarters at Verplanck's Point [north of New York City on the Hudson River]. Whenever her health permitted, she followed the army; and it is represented that her presence and cheerful manners did much to diffuse contentment and enliven dreary scenes. The soldiers could not murmur at privations which she endured without complaint. Sad it is, that no record remains of the ministrations of women in thus softening war's grim features. The good they did, however, was at the time acknowledged with respectful gratitude. There is reason to believe that General Knox often deferred to his wife's judgment, regarding her as a superior being; and it is said that her influence and superiority were owned by Washington himself. Her mind was undoubtedly of a high order, and her character a remarkable one. She appears to have possessed an ascendency over all with whom she associated. After the close of the struggle, while General Knox held the office of Secretary of War, his wife's position was next to that of Mrs. Washington, whom she advised in matters of ceremony. Mrs. Knox had a taste for the management and show of public life, and was a leader of the ton [fashion] in the social circles at the seat of government.[110]

Date	Events
1756	Born in Boston
June 16, 1774	Marries Henry Knox. Lucy is basically disowned by her family, who are British loyalists.
April 19, 1775	Lucy and Henry flee Boston and their bookstore there, after the battles of Lexington and Concord
March 1776	Lucy's family returns to England after the British evacuate Boston
Winter 1777/78	Lucy joins her husband at Valley Forge, and like Martha Washington, spends much of her time sewing for the men and tending to the sick
1778	After the battle of Monmouth, Lucy joins her husband in encampment at Pluckemin, New Jersey. Henry operated an artillery school there.
February 18, 1779	A grand ball held by Henry and Lucy Knox, with almost 400 people in attendance, including General

[110] *The Women of the American Revolution, Volume 1*, by Elizabeth Fries Ellet (Baker and Scribner, 1819)

Date	Events
	Washington
October 1781	Battle of Yorktown
Post-war	The couple live first in Newburgh, New York, and then in the Boston Area. Henry is in charge of disbanding the army.
March 8, 1785 - September 12, 1789	Henry acts as Secretary of War under the Articles of Confederation
September 12, 1789	Henry becomes Secretary of War in Washington's cabinet
1795	Henry and Lucy retire to Montpelier, in Thomaston, Maine
October 25, 1806	Henry dies from a chicken bone lodged in his throat
1824	Dies at Montpelier

Sybil Ludington

Sybil Ludington was born in 1761 in Kent, New York. Her father was Henry Ludington, who would go on to take command of the Seventh Militia of Dutchess County, New York during the Revolutionary War.

On April 25, 1777, the British landed at Compo Beach, Westport, Connecticut with a force of 2,000, with the intention of destroying the Colonial stores at Danbury, Connecticut.

A rider was dispatched to Colonel Ludington's home to apprise him of the situation in Danbury, and to request that he muster the militia. The rider arrived at Ludington's home, and delivered the message, but claimed his horse (and he himself) were too tired to go on. Since Colonel Ludington needed to go about the business of organizing the militia as they trickled it, the job of calling in the militia fell to his 16 year old daughter. So, on April 26, 1777 at night, she embarked on a 40 mile ride to warn people of the area that the British had attacked Danbury, Connecticut. Her travels went in a clockwise circle, and included Carmel, Mahopac, Kent Cliffs, Farmers Mills, Stormville and then back home. In 1935, the New York State Education department erected markers along her route, which included:

    Ludington, on Route 52 north of old mill
    Carmel, on Route 6 along lake Gleneida
    Mahopac, at junction of Route 6 and Route 6N
    Mahopac Falls, at junction of Hill St. and Route 6N
    Kent Cliffs, at junction Rt. 301 and Peekskill Hollow Road
    Mead Corner at junction Rt. 301 and Farmers Mill Rd.
    Stormville, at junction Routes 216 and 52
    Patterson, at burial place near Presbyterian Church[111]

---

[111] *Putnam County Courier*, (Carmel, N.Y.), June 30, 1960

The militia was successfully mustered, and although it was too late to save Danbury, the militia harassed the British column as they retreated. (Picture: "Sybil Ludington, 1776", c. 1850 by Granger[112])

There are several challenges to researching the Sybil Ludington story. First, there are many spellings of her name, including Sybil, Sybyl and Sibbell (on her tombstone). Second, there don't seem to be any contemporary sources which discuss her ride in detail. In 1907, her great-nephew Louis S. Patrick recounted the story in a paper he wrote, and in the same year, Willis Fletcher Johnson recounted the ride in his book *Colonel Henry Ludington: A Memoir*:

> The messenger from Danbury could ride no more, and there was no neighbor within call. In this emergency he turned to his daughter Sibyl, who, a few days before, had passed her sixteenth birthday, and bade her to take a horse, ride for the men, and tell them to be at his house by daybreak. One who even now rides from Carmel to Cold Spring will find rugged and dangerous roads, with lonely stretches. Imagination only can picture what it was a century and a quarter ago, on a dark night, with reckless bands of "Cowboys" and "Skinners" abroad in the land. But the child performed her task, clinging to a man's saddle, and guiding her steed with only a hempen halter, as she rode through the night, bearing the news of the sack of Danbury. There is no extravagance in comparing her ride with that of Paul Revere and its midnight message. Nor was her errand less efficient than his. By daybreak, thanks to her daring, nearly the whole regiment was mustered before her father's house at Fredericksburgh, and an hour or two

[112] Public domain.

later was on the march for vengeance on the raiders. They were a motley company, some without arms, some half dressed, but all filled with a certain berserk rage. That night they reached Redding, and joined Arnold, Wooster and Silliman. The next morning they encountered the British at Ridgefield. They were short of ammunition and were outnumbered by the British three to one. But they practiced the same tactics that Paul Revere's levies at Lexington and Concord found so effective. Their scattering sharpshooter fire from behind trees and fences and stone walls, harassed the British sorely, and made their retreat to their ships at Compo resemble a rout. [113]

In 1912, Fred C. Warner wrote the following poem memorializing the exploit:

On An April Night - 1777
The showers fell gently that April night:
On town and country alike they fell,
As the Ludington family by candle light
Settled down for an evening they loved so well.
Through the rain and darkness a horseman came;
From Danbury town to the west he had sped.
"Come over and help use, our homes are aflame,
Call out your militia!" the horseman said.
The steed was exhausted, the rider spent
For the way was long and the pace was hard;
Who was there to see that the word was sent
To hundreds of men of Ludington's Guard?
Who would bear tidings of anguish and fear
To the farms and hamlets o'er valley and hill?
The mission was urgent, its meaning was clear!
Up spake young Sybil, "Please, Daddy, I will".
The big bay colt she had broken to ride
Was saddled and bridled and led from the stall;
In jeans and loose jacket she mounted astride,
The country folk would be hearing her call.
Along the trail by the river she road through the night
Spreading on down the valley the news and alarm
That a city was burning to come enter the fight
From every cottage and hamlet and farm.

[113] *Colonel Henry Ludington: A Memoir,* by Willis Fletcher Johnson (Lavinia Elizabeth Ludington and Charles Henry Ludington, 1907)

By the Lake of Gleneida and Mahopac's shore
Where fisherman's loved ones in slumber were still,
Now woke to the chant of the message she bore,
"Muster at once at Ludington's Mill!"
To the west and then north she soon made her way;
The families of miners next heard her shrill call;
Through the thick of the forest where bandits held sway
She sped on regardless of danger and ail.
Ever onward advancing through the dark and the rain,
As she came to the northernmost point of her way.
Her steed was quick in response to her rein
And brought her back home ere the dawn of the day.
We know well the story how the militiamen came.
How the British were conquered and freedom was won;
And our people today are proud of the name
As they tell of the fame of Sybil Ludington[114] (Fred C. Warner, 1912)

Date	Events
April 5, 1761	Born Anna Hyatt Huntington in Kent, New York
April 18, 1775	Paul Revere's Ride
1776	Colonel Henry Ludington takes command of the Seventh Militia of Dutchess County, New York
April 25, 1777	The British land at at Compo Beach, Westport, Connecticut, and head towards Colonial stores at Danbury, Connecticut
April 26, 1777	16-year old Sybil rides 40 miles to warn people that the British had attacked Danbury, Connecticut. Her travels include Carmel, NY, Mahopac, Kent Cliffs, Farmers Mills, Stormville and home
1784	Marries Edmond Ogden. They would have 1 child.
1792	The family moves to Unadilla, New York
February 26, 1839	Dies in Catskill, New York
1907	Willis Fletcher Johnson puts the story on paper in 1907, at the request of Sybil's descendants
1912	Fred C. Warner writes the poem On an April Night 1777
1935	Markers are erected along her route by New York State Education Department

[114] *Putnam County Courier*, (Carmel, N.Y.), June 30, 1960

Date	Events
1961	A statue is erected in Sybil's honor near Carmel, New York
March 25, 1975	8 cent "Contributors to the Cause" stamp issued by the U.S. Postal Service

Margaret Catherine Moore (Catherine Moore Barry)

Date	Events
November 29, 1752	Born (possibly in Ireland, or near Spartanburg, SC)
1767	Marries Andrew Barry. The would live on a plantation called Walnut Grove, near Spartanburg (Roebuck), South Carolina, and have 11 children[115]
January 17, 1781	• Warns the local militia that the British are coming before the Battle of Cowpens (South Carolina) • Brigadier General Daniel Morgan defeats Colonel Banastre Tarleton and the British at the Battle of Cowpens
June 17, 1811	Captain Andrew Barry dies
September 29, 1823	Dies in Spartanburg, SC
October 1, 1901	Kate Barry Chapter of the DAR established in Spartanburg, SC
1961	Parts of Walnut Grove pass from ownership by the Moore family to the Spartanburg County Foundation "in a special trust with the Spartanburg County Historical Association"
1976	Moore Building at the University of North Carolina at Greensboro is named

Our subject here is referred to by several names, including Margaret Catherine[116] Moore, Catherine Moore Barry and Kate Barry. Biographical information about her is scarce – some sources say she was born in Ireland, some in Pennsylvania, and some in Spartanburg, South Carolina. Most agree that she was born in 1752.

When the Revolutionary War started, her husband, Andrew Barry, became a captain in the Colonial militia. Kate became a

---

[115] Some sources say 10 children
[116] Sometimes spelled "Kathryn"

spy and scout, passing on information about British troop movements in her area to Colonial officials. According to one story, British soldiers came to her house once in search of her husband, and when she refused to tell them where he was, she was put to the lash. Another story says that she escaped from the British by swimming across a creek or river.

She is most famous as the "heroine of the battle of Cowpens", when she informed Brigadier-General Daniel Morgan (or her husband, Captain Barry in some versions) that the British (led by Colonel Banastre Tarleton) were on the march towards their position. The ensuing Battle of Cowpens was a great Colonial victory, and was the beginning of the end for the British occupation of South Carolina.

Walnut Grove Plantation has been restored, and is open to the public.

Walnut Grove, Roebuck, Spartanburg County, South Carolina[117]

---

[117] Library of Congress http://www.loc.gov/pictures/item/sc0763.photos.150919p/

Molly Pitcher (Mary Ludwig Hays)

Date	Events
c. October 13, 1754	Born in Trenton, NJ
1770	Marries William Hays[118]; the couple settles in Carlisle, PA
December 1, 1775	William Hays joins Proctor's 4th Pennsylvania Artillery
Winter 1777/78	Mary joins William at Valley Forge, where she operates as a "camp follower", doing laundry, cleaning, cooking etc.
June 28, 1778	Battle of Monmouth, New Jersey. Mary ("Molly") may – or may not – have taken her husband's place at a cannon after her husband was stricken by heat exhaustion (or wounded)
1786	William Hays dies in Carlisle, PA
1793	Marries John McCauley
c. 1807	McCauley disappears
February 21, 1822	The Commonwealth of Pennsylvania awards Mary McCauley an annual pension of $40 "for her services during the Civil War"
January 22, 1832	Dies in Carlisle, PA
1928	"Molly Pitcher" overprint stamp issued
1943	Liberty ship SS Molly Pitcher launched, and is torpedoed west of Lisbon
1978	Molly Pitcher post card issued

One of the enduring legends of the Battle of Monmouth is of a young women nicknamed "Molly Pitcher", who provided water to thirsty Continentals on the battlefield, as well as to artillery crews to swab their guns. She may have been one Mary Ludwig Hays, married to a local Continental artillery man. Further legends say that when he went down injured,

---

[118] Or "John" Hays, in other accounts

219

"Molly" took his place at the cannon. The full truth of the matter may never be known.

It should be pointed out that Molly Pitcher is sometimes confused with Margaret Corbin (and vice-versa), who performed a similar heroic act at the Battle for Fort Washington. To make matters worse, by women are sometimes referred to as "Molly".

"The Heroine on Monmouth. Molly Pitcher ... June 28, 1778"[119]

An example of the confusion surrounding Molly Pitcher can be seen in the poem on the next page, from a newspaper article published in 1902[120]. Note that the name of the gunner is "Pitcher".

---

[119] Library of Congress http://www.loc.gov/pictures/item/2006691580/
[120] *Pullman Herald*, (Pullman, W.T. [Wash.]), July 5, 1902

Pitcher the gunner is brisk and young;
He's a lightsome heart and a merry tongue,
An ear like a fox, an eye like a hawk,
A foot that would sooner run than walk,
And a hand that can touch the linstock
    home
As the lightning darts from the thunder-
    dome.
He hates a tory; he loves a fight;
The roll of the drum is his heart's delight;
And three things rule the gunner's life;
His country, his gun, and his Irish wife.
    Oh, Molly, with your eyes so blue!
    Oh, Molly, Molly, here's to you!
    Sweet Honor's roll will aye be richer
    To hold the name of Molly Pitcher.

A bullet comes singing over the brow,
And—Pitcher's gun is silent now.
The brazen throat that roared his will,
The shout of his warlike joy, is still.
The black lips curl, but they shoot no
    flame,
And the voice that cries on the gunner's
    name
Finds only it's echo where he lies
With his steadfast face turned up to the
    skies.
    Oh, Molly, Molly, where he lies
    His last look meets your faithful eyes;
    His last thought sinks from love to love
    Of your darling face that bends above.

"No one to serve in Pitcher's stead?
Wheel back the gun!" the captain said;
When, like a flash, before him stood
A figure dashed with smoke and blood,
With streaming hair, and eyes of flame,
And lips that falter the gunner's name.
"Wheel back his gun, that never yet
His fighting duty did forget?
His voice shall speak, though he lie dead;

I'll serve my husband's gun!" she said.
    Oh, Molly, now your hour is come!
    Up, girl, and strike the linstock home!
    Leap out, swift ball! Away! away!
    Avenge the gunner's death to-day!

All day the great guns barked and roared;
All day the big balls screeched and soared;
All day, 'mid the sweating gunners grim,
Who toiled in their smoke-shroud dense and
    dim,
Sweet Molly labored with courage high,
With steady hand and watchful eye,
Till the day was ours, and the sinking sun
Looked down on the field of Monmouth won,
And Molly standing beside her gun.
    Now, Molly, rest your weary arm!
    Safe, Molly, all is safe from harm,
    Now, woman, bow your aching head,
    And weep in sorrow o'er your dead!

Next day on that field so hardly won,
Stately and calm stands Washington,
And looks where our gallant Greene doth
    lead
A figure clad in motley weed—
A soldier's cap and a soldier's coat
Masking a woman's petticoat.
He greets our Molly in kindly wise;
He bids her raise her fearful eyes;
And now he hails her before them all
Comrade and soldier, whate'er befall.
"And since she has played a man's full part,
A man's reward for her loyal heart!
And Sergeant Molly Pitcher's name
Be writ henceforth on the shield of fame!"
    Oh, Molly, with your eyes so blue!
    Oh, Molly, Molly, here's to you!
    Sweet Honor's roll will aye be richer
    To hold the name of Molly Pitcher.
        —Laura E. Richards, in St. Nicholas.

There are many versions of the Molly Pitcher story. Below is one from 1905, culled from earlier sources:

We come now to the period when the episode occurred which made her famous. To prevent the movement of the British on New York, Washington marched his troops again into New Jersey, and the battle of Monmouth was fought on the 28th of June, 1778. At that time Molly Hays was a young woman of twenty-four years.

According to Alexander Hamilton and Colonel William Irvine, the decisive battle of Monmouth continued from eleven o'clock in the morning until half past four in the afternoon. The day was one of the hottest of the year. Lossing says the battle lasted from nine o'clock in the morning until night. Fifty soldiers are said to have died of thirst, and the tongues of many to have been so greatly swollen as to protrude from the mouth. While the battle was in progress Molly carried water for the thirsting soldiers from a neighboring spring, which is still pointed out on the historic spot. Back and forth she went, under shelter or under fire, supplying the much needed water. Possibly, as is stated by some, it was carried in the cannonniers' bucket. In whatever way it was carried, the sight of Molly with her "pitcher" was a welcome sight to the weary and thirsty soldiers.

Molly's husband, as will be remembered, had served for one year in Proctor's Artillery, and though now an infantryman, had been detailed as a gunner in a battery that was engaged. Doubtless Molly was never out of sight of that battery. As she was coming toward the smoking lines with water she saw a soldier lying at his gun, whom she thought to be her husband, and hurrying on she found her husband wounded, and the dead man one of his comrades. It is stated that the cannon was ordered to the rear, and would have been taken off the field, had not Molly bravely sprung to her husband's place, and so kept the gun in action. Her husband recovered, but lived only a few years after the close of the war.

One of Molly's strong characteristics, exhibited in many and various ways, was her readiness to help others in time of need. Opportunity was all that was necessary. She was intensely interested in the war. A warm patriot and a warmer hater of the redcoats, she could not see the poor soldiers in the heat and dust of battle suffering from thirst, without exposing her own life, if necessary, in their relief. How grateful must Molly's "pitcher" have been to those thirsting men, and how astonishing her bravery, as she seized the rammer and worked like an Amazon to save her husband's gun. She was dubbed "sergeant," by the soldiers, and was also called "Major Molly."

> Moll Pitcher she stood by her gun,
> And rammed the charges home, sir,
> And thus on Monmouth's bloody field,
> A sergeant did become sir.

How long, in the smoke and din of battle Molly stood by her gun on that hot and terrible day we do not know. But what time she carried water must be credited to the brave woman, as well as the time she was engaged with the battery.[121]

A bit closer to the source, the redoubtable Joseph Plumb Martin was an eye-witness to the event, as noted in his *Narrative:*

One little incident happened, during the heat of the cannonade, which I was eye-witness to, and which I think would be unpardonable not to mention. A woman whose husband belonged to the Artillery, and who was then attached to a piece in the engagement, attended with her husband at the piece the whole time; while in the act of reaching a cartridge and having one of her feet as far before the other as she could step, a cannon shot from the enemy passed directly between her legs without doing any other damage than carrying away all the lower part of her petticoat, looking at it with apparent unconcern, she observed that it was lucky it did not pass a little higher, for in that case it might have carried away something else, and continued her occupation.[122]

Molly Pitcher – a woman who fought for her country in the American Revolution.

---

[121] *A Short History of Molly Pitcher, the Heroine of the Battle of Monmouth*, by John B. Landis (The Cornman Printing Company, 1905)

[122] *A Narrative of Some of the Adventures, Dangers and Sufferings of a Revolutionary Soldier*, by Joseph Plumb Martin (Glazier, Masters & Co., 1830)

Esther de Berdt Reed

Esther de Berdt Reed was born of Huguenot stock in London in 1746. She married lawyer and future soldier and politician Joseph Reed in 1770, and they soon emigrated to the United States. The couple settled in Philadelphia.[123]

A number of letters written by Esther are still extant, including this one in which she commented about local Philadelphia ladies after the arrival of the Reeds in Philadelphia.

> The belles of the city were there. In general, the ladies are pretty, but no beauties; they all stoop, like country girls.[124] (November 14, 1770)

Although Esther had spent the first 25 years of her life in England, by 1775, she was entirely in support of the American cause in the coming War, as these excerpts from her letters of the time indicate:

> I think the cause in which he [James Reed, who was an aide to General Washington] is engaged, so just, so glorious, and I hope will be so victorious, that private interest and pleasure may and ought to be given up, without a murmur. But where sleep all our friends in England? Where sleep the virtue and justice of the English nation? Will nothing rouse them, or are they so few in number, and small in consequence, that though awake, their voice cannot be heard for the multitude of our enemies.[125] (Sept. 8, 1775)

---

[123] Portrait by Charles Willson Peale (1741-1827). Frick Art Reference Library. Public domain.

[124] *The Life of Esther De Berdt: Afterwards Esther Reed, of Pennsylvania*, by William Bradford Reed (C. Sherman, printer, 1853)

It seems now to depend on the reception of our last Petition from the Congress to the King; if that should be so considered as to lay a foundation for negotiation, we may be again reconciled,—if not, I imagine We Shall Declare For Independence, and exert our utmost to defend ourselves. This proposition would have alarmed almost every person on the Continent a twelvemonth ago, but now the general voice is, if the Ministry and Nation will drive us to it, we must do it, rather than submit, after so many public resolutions to the contrary.[126] (October 28, 1775)

Thus, in a mere five years, the English lass had turned into a Colonial Patriot.

Her husband answered the call to arms in 1775 when he became an aide on George Washington's staff, with the rank of colonel. In 1776, he became Adjutant General of the Continental army.

The reason for including Esther de Berdt Reed in our list of heroines of the Revolution is because of her efforts in 1780 to have the Ladies Association of Philadelphia raise money to help the Continental Army. An excerpt from a letter from Esther to General Washington on July 4, 1776 underscores the astonishing success of the effort:

ESTHER REED TO WASHINGTON.
Philadelphia, July 4th, 1780.

Sir,
The subscription set on foot by the ladies of this city for the use of the soldiery, is so far completed as to induce me to transmit to your Excellency an account of the money I have received, and which, although it has answered our expectations, it does not equal our wishes, but I am persuaded will be received as a proof

---

[125] *The Life of Esther De Berdt: Afterwards Esther Reed*, of Pennsylvania, by William Bradford Reed (C. Sherman, printer, 1853)
[126] *The Life of Esther De Berdt: Afterwards Esther Reed*, of Pennsylvania, by William Bradford Reed (C. Sherman, printer, 1853)

of our zeal for the great cause of America and our esteem and gratitude for those who so bravely defend it.

The amount of the subscription is 200,580 dollars, and £625 6s. 8d. in specie, which makes in the whole in paper money 300,634 dollars.

The ladies are anxious for the soldiers to receive the benefit of it, and wait your directions how it can best be disposed of. We expect some considerable additions from the country and have also wrote to the other States in hopes the ladies there will adopt similar plans, to render it more general and beneficial.

With the utmost pleasure I offer any farther attention and care in my power to complete the execution of the design, and shall be happy to accomplish it agreeably to the intention of the donors and your wishes on the subject.

The ladies of my family join me in their respectful compliments and sincerest prayer for your health, safety, and success. I have the honour to be, with the highest respect,

Your obedient humble servant,[127]

The original intention of the Ladies Association of Philadelphia had been to give the money to the troops to spend as they wished. Washington suggested an alternate plan – could the ladies use the money to purchase linen shirts for the men? The letter below shows that Washington had to make the suggestion twice:

I received this morning a letter from the General [Washington], and he still continues his opinion that the money in my hands should be laid out in linen; he says no supplies he has at present, or has a prospect of, are any way adequate to the wants of the army; his letter is, I think, a little formal, as if he was hurt by our asking his opinion a second time, and our not following his directions, after desiring to give them. The letter is very

---

[127] *The Life of Esther De Berdt: Afterwards Esther Reed*, of Pennsylvania, by William Bradford Reed (C. Sherman, printer, 1853)

complaisant, and I shall now endeavour to get the shirts made as soon as possible. (August 22, 1780)

The Ladies Association soon kicked into high gear, and over 2,000 shirts had been made or procured by December of 1780. Esther died on September 18, 1780, from complications from smallpox and dysentery.

Date	Events
October 22, 1746	Born in London
1763 or 1764	Meets Joseph Reed, then a law student at the Temple. They become engaged.
c. February 7, 1765	Joseph Reed sails for America. He wouldn't return to England for 5 years.
1766	Daughters of Liberty formed; Esther would later be a member
March 14, 1770	Joesph Reed returns to England
May 22, 1770	Marries lawyer Joseph Reed at St. Luke's Church in London
October 26, 1770	Joseph and Esther arrive in Philadelphia
Fall 1774	Joseph Reed is elected as a member of the First Continental Congress in Philadelphia
1776	Joseph Reed becomes Adjutant General of the Continental army
September 1777	Esther leaves her home near Philadelphia as the British occupy the city. She returns after the British evacuate the city in July 1778.
December 1778	Joesph Reed is elected President of the Executive Council of the State of Pennsylvania
June 10, 1780	Publishes broadside *The Sentiments of an American Woman*, which appeals to women to contribute to the war effort
1780	Ladies Association of Philadelphia raises $300,000 from 1,645 contributors[128] (!)
September 18,	Dies In Philadelphia, PA from complications from

---

[128] *The Life of Esther De Berdt: Afterwards Esther Reed*, of Pennsylvania, by William Bradford Reed (C. Sherman, printer, 1853)

Date	Events
1780	smallpox and dysentery
1853	*The Life of Esther De Berdt: Afterwards Esther Reed, of Pennsylvania* is published by her grandson William Bradford Reed

Esther's primary written legacy, other then her letters, is her *Sentiments of An American Woman* tract of 1780. Some excerpts are presented here.

IN the commencement of actual war, the Women of America manifested a firm resolution to contribute as much as could depend on them, to the deliverance of their country. Animated by the purest patriotism, they are sensible of sorrow at this day, in not offering more than barren wishes for the success of so glorious a Revolution. They aspire to render themselves more really useful; and this sentiment is universal from the north to the south of the Thirteen United States. Our ambition is kindled by the same of those heroines of antiquity, who have rendered their sex illustrious, and have proved to the universe, that, if the weakness of our Constitution, if opinion and manners did not forbid us to march to glory by the same paths as the Men, we should at least equal, and sometimes surpass them in our love for the public good...

...The situation of our soldiery has been represented to me; the evils inseparable from war, and the firm and generous spirit which has enabled them to support these. But it has been said, that they may apprehend, that, in the course of a long war, the view of their distresses may be lost, and their services be forgotten. Forgotten! never; I can answer in the name of all my sex. Brave Americans, your disinterestedness, your courage, and your constancy will always be dear to America, as long as she shall preserve her virtue.

We know that at a distance from the theatre of war, if we enjoy any tranquility, it is the fruit of your watchings, your labours, your dangers. If I live happy in the midst of my family; if my husband cultivates his field, and reaps his harvest in peace; if, surrounded with my children, I myself nourish the youngest, and press it to my bosom, without being afraid of feeling myself separated from it, by a ferocious enemy; if the house in which we dwell; if our barns, our orchards are safe at the present time from the hands of those incendiaries, it is to you that we owe it. And shall we hesitate to evidence to you our gratitude? Shall we hesitate to wear a clothing more simple; hair dressed less elegant, while at the price of this small privation, we shall deserve your benedictions. Who, amongst us, will not renounce with the highest pleasure, those vain ornaments, when-she shall consider that the valiant defenders of America will be able to draw some advantage from the money which she may have laid out in these; that they will be better defended from the rigours of the seasons, that after their painful toils, they will receive some extraordinary and unexpected relief; that these presents will perhaps be valued by them at a greater price, when they will have it in their power to say: This is the offering of the Ladies. The time is arrived to display the same sentiments which animated us at the beginning of the Revolution, when we renounced the use of teas, however agreeable to our taste, rather than receive them from our persecutors; when we made it appear to them that we placed former necessaries in the rank of superfluities, when our liberty was interested; when our republican and laborious hands spun the flax, prepared the linen intended for the use of our soldiers; when exiles and fugitives we supported with courage all the evils which are the concomitants of war. Let us not lose a moment; let us be engaged to offer the homage of our gratitude at the altar of military valour, and you, our brave deliverers, while mercenary slaves combat to cause you to share with them, the irons with which they are loaded, receive with a free hand our offering, the purest which can be presented to your virtue, By An AMERICAN WOMAN.[129]

---

[129] http://www-personal.umd.umich.edu/~ppennock/doc-Sentiments%20of%20An %20American%20Woman.htm

Betsy Ross

Betsy Ross was born Elizabeth Phoebe Griscom in Philadelphia, PA on January 1, 1752. She was the 8th of what would be 17 children (only 9 survived childhood). As was the case with many in Philadelphia at the time, the family were strict Quakers.

As a young woman, Betsy was apprenticed to an upholsterer named William Webster. As an upholsterer, she learned to do all types of sewing (not just furniture and curtains). In November 1773, knowing her family wouldn't approved, she eloped with a fellow apprentice named John Ross. Ross was the son of Anglican priest (and later assistant rector at Christ Church) Aeneas Ross.[130]

Betsy was expelled from the Society of friends. She and her husband began attending Christ Church, where she would have met George Washington. The Ross family had pew number 12 in Christ Church.

Betsy and John set up their own upholstery business. When the Revolutionary War broke out, John joined the Pennsylvania Provincial Militia. He was killed on January 21, 1776, in action against the British. Betsy continued operating the upholstery business, and thus was there on the fateful day in the Spring of 1776 when she was visited in her shop by

---

[130] Image: Library of Congress http://www.loc.gov/pictures/item/94507644/

George Washington and Colonel George Ross, the uncle of her departed husband.

Date	Events
c. 1740	The front part of the building (now the Betsy Ross House) at 239 Arch Street in Philadelphia is built
January 1, 1752	Born Elizabeth Griscom in Philadelphia, Pennsylvania
November 1773	Elopes with John Ross, an apprentice working at the upholstery shop where Betsy worked. She is soon expelled from the Society of friends. She and her husband begin attending Christ Church, where she meets George Washington.
1776/79	Betsy occupies the building (now the Betsy Ross House) at 239 Arch Street in Philadelphia
January 1776	War with Great Britain breaks out and John Ross, a member of the Pennsylvania Provincial Militia, is mortally wounded. He dies on January 21, 1776.
Spring 1776	Betsy Ross may (or may not) have sewn the first flag of the United States, at the request of George Washington
1777	British soldiers are bivouacked in Betsy's home
May 29, 1777	Betsy receives a payment from the Pennsylvania State Navy Board for making flags
June 14, 1777	Flag Act of 1777 is passed by the Continental Congress. "Resolved, That the flag of the thirteen United States be thirteen stripes, alternate red and white; that the union be thirteen stars, white in a blue field, representing a new constellation."
June 15, 1777	Marries Joseph Ashburn at Old Swedes Church
March 1782	Joseph Ashburn dies in custody of the British
May 1783	Marries John Claypoole, who had been in prison in England with Joseph Ashburn
c. 1784	Betsy and John Claypoole join the Society of Free Quakers, a group which supports the American Revolution
1793	Betsy's mother, father, and sister die from yellow fever
1812	Betsy's daughter Clarissa moves in with Betsy and John, and helps Betsy with the upholstery business

Date	Events
1813	Betsy's daughter Mary Young Pickersgill sews the huge "Star Spangled Banner" flag
September 12/14, 1814	Mary's flag flies over Fort McHenry in Baltimore Harbor, and is seen by Francis Scott Key
1817	Claypoole dies
1827	Betsy retires from the upholstery business
1833	Betsy is completely blind
January 30, 1836	Dies in Philadelphia, Pennsylvania, and is initially buried in the Free Quaker burial ground at South 5th St. near Locust[131]
1870	Betsy Ross's grandson, William J. Canby, presents a paper to the Historical Society of Pennsylvania. He claims that Betsy "made with her hands the first flag" of the United States.
1898	American Flag House and Betsy Ross Memorial Association established
June 14, 1937	All rooms of the restored Betsy Ross house opened to the public
1941	Atwater Kent purchases two properties to the west of the house to create a "civic garden"
January 1, 1952	3¢ stamp issued by the Post Office commemorating the 200th anniversary of the birth of Betsy Ross
1974	The courtyard of the Betsy Ross house is renovated, and a fountain is added
1976	The remains of Betsy Ross and John Claypoole are moved to the courtyard west of the house
April 1976	Betsy Ross Bridge across the Delaware open. It runs from Philadelphia, Pennsylvania to Pennsauken, New Jersey.

The source of many legends are lost in the mists of time, but the legend about Betsy Ross sewing the first flag can be traced exactly. The grandson of Betsy Ross, William Canby, read a paper to the Historical Society of Pennsylvania in March 1870. The paper was entitled *The History of the Flag of the United States*, and it contained all of the elements of the story as we know it today:

---

[131] She would later be re-interred at Mt. Moriah Cemetery, and in 1976, she was re-interred in the courtyard of the Betsy Ross House

- During the Spring of 1776, Colonel George Ross, uncle of Betsy's deceased husband John, and General George Washington visited Betsy's shop, announcing they were a committee from Congress
- They asked her if she could produce a flag to the specifications that Ross gave her
- Betsy suggested some improvements to the design, which were approved. One of the improvements was to use 5-point stars on the flag, instead of the six that were on the design drawing
- Betsy was subsequently given a painting of the new design, as well as an example of the stitching to be used
- Other designs had been given to other seamstresses
- Betsy's flag was run up the mast of a ship at a nearby wharf, and approved by the committee, who then presented the flag to Congress, who also approved it
- With the help of 100 pounds seed money, Betsy was given an order for "unlimited" flags by the Continental government

Here is an excerpt from the original paper.

Sitting sewing in her shop one day with her girls around her, several gentlemen entered. She recognized one of these as the uncle of her deceased husband, Col. GEORGE ROSS, a delegate from Pennsylvania to Congress. She also knew the handsome form and features of the dignified, yet graceful and polite Commander in Chief, who, while he was yet COLONEL WASHINGTON had visited her shop both professionally and socially many times, (a friendship caused by her connection with the Ross family). They announced themselves as a committee of congress, and stated that they had been appointed to prepare a flag, and asked her if she thought she could make one, to which she replied, with her usual modesty and self reliance, that "she did not know but she could try; she had never made one but if the pattern were shown to her she had not doubt of her ability to do it." The committee were shown into her back parlor, the room back of the shop, and Col. Ross produced a drawing, roughly made, of the proposed flag. It was defective to the clever eye of Mrs Ross and unsymetrical, and she offered suggestions which Washington and the committee readily approved.

What all these suggestions were we cannot definitely determine, but they were of sufficient importance to involve an alteration and re-drawing of the design, which was then and there done by General George Washington, in pencil, in her back parlor. One of the alterations had reference to the shape of the stars. In the drawing they were made with six points.

Mrs Ross at once said that this was wrong; the stars should be five pointed; they were aware of that, but thought there would be some difficulty in making a five pointed star. "Nothing easier" was her prompt reply and folding a piece of paper in the proper manner, with one clip of her ready scissors she quickly displayed to their astonished vision the five pointed star; which accordingly took its place in the national standard. General Washington was the active one in making the design, the others having little or nothing to do with it. When it was completed, it was given to William Barrett, painter, to paint...

The committee suggested Mrs Ross to call at a certain hour at the counting house of one of their number, a shipping merchant, on the wharf. Mrs Ross was punctual to the appointment. The gentleman drew out of a chest an old ship's color, which he loaned her to show her how the sewing was done, and also the drawing painted by Barrett. Other designs had been prepared by the committee and one or two of them were placed in the hands of other seamstresses to be made. Betsy Ross went diligently to work upon her flag, carefully examining the peculiar stitch in the old ship's color, which had been given her as a specimen, and recognizing, with the eye of a good mechanic its important characteristics, strength and elasticity.

The flag was soon finished, and Betsy returned it, the first 'Star Spangled Banner' that ever floated upon the breeze, to her employer. It was run up to the peak of one of his ships lying at the wharf, and received the unamimous approval of the committee and of a little group of bystanders looking on, and the same day

234

was carried into the State House and laid before Congress, with a report from the committee.

The next day Col. Ross called upon Betsy, and informed her that her work had been approved and her flag adopted; and he now requested her to turn her whole attention to the manufacture of flags, and gave her an unlimited order for as many as she could make; desiring her to go out forthwith and buy all the "bunting and tack" in the city, and make flags as fast as possible. Here was astounding mews [sic] to Betsy! Her largest ideas of business heretofore had been confined to the furnishing of one or two houses at a time with beds, curtains and carpets; and she had only recently been depressed with the prospect of losing much of this limited business by reason of the high prices of materials, and the consequent retrenchment by citizens in luxuries that could be dispensed with. She sat ruminating upon her sudden good fortune some minutes before it occurred to her that she had not the means to make the extensive purchases required by the order; and, therefore, she would be utterly helpless to fill it; for these were the days of cash transactions, and such a thing as a poor person getting credit for a large amount of goods was altogether unheard of. Here was a dilemma. What was she to do? Like many others, she began already to doubt her good fortune and to dash her rising hopes with the reflections, "this is too good luck for me, it cannot be". Rising superior to this, however, she said to herself, "We are not creatures of luck: have I not found that the Good One has never deserted me, and He will not now. I will buy all the bunting I can, and make it into these flags, and will explain to Mr. Ross why I cannot get anymore. He will, no doubt, give orders to others, and so I shall lose a large part of this business: but I must be satisfied with a moderate share of it, and grateful too." So she went to work. Scarcely had she finished her cogitations when Col. Ross re-entered the shop. "It was very thoughtless of me" he remarked, "when I was just here now, that I did not offer to supply you with the means for making these purchases; it might inconvenience you" he said delicately, "to pay out so much cash at once, here is something to begin with" (giving her a one hundred pound note) "and you must draw on me at sight for what ever you require."

Mrs Ross was now effectively set up in the business of flag and color making for the government; through all her after life, which was a long, useful and eventful one, she "never knew what it was," to use her own expression, "to want employment," this business (flag-making for the government) remaining with her and in her family for many years. She was afterwards twice married; once to Joseph Ashbourne, a shipmaster in the merchant services, by whom she had one daughter, named Eliza, and after his death to John Claypoole.[132] (*The History of the Flag of the United States* by William Canby; A Paper read before the Historical Society of Pennsylvania (March 1870))

Betsy would marry twice more. Her second husband, Joseph Ashburn would die in March 1782 in an English prison. He had been captured by a British Royal Navy frigate in 1780, and charged with treason. He died in the Old Mill Prison, in England, never seeing his wife again.

Betsy heard the news about her husband's death from John Claypoole, who had served time with Joseph Ashburn in prison. In May 1783, Claypoole and Betsy were married. Betsy now returned to her Quaker roots, joining (with her husband) the Society of Free Quakers, a group that had supported the American Revolution. Betsy remained married to John Claypoole until 1817, when he died after a long illness.

The now-blind Betsy Claypoole died on January 30, 1836 in Philadelphia. She is now buried in the courtyard of the Betsy Ross House at 239 Arch Street, Philadelphia, PA 19106.

In April 1976, the Betsy Ross Bridge across the Delaware opened. It runs from Philadelphia, Pennsylvania to Pennsauken, New Jersey.

---

[132] http://www.ushistory.org/betsy/more/canby.htm

Betsy Ross House in Philadelphia

Mercy Otis Warren

Date	Events
September 14, 1728	Born in Barnstable, Massachusetts
1754	Marries James Warren, sheriff of Plymouth County, Massachusetts. They would have five children.
1765/77	Her husband James Warren serves as a member of the Massachusetts House (Speaker of the House in 1775)
1769	Her brother James Otis is beaten by British revenue officers
1772	Publishes *The Adulateur,* a satire regarding Governor Thomas Hutchinson ("Rapatio") of Massachusetts, using a pseudonym
November 1772	Assists in setting up the first Committees of Correspondence in Massachusetts. In time, the committees would play a large role in summoning the First Continental Congress
1773	Publishes *The Defeat*, also targeting Thomas Hutchinson ("Rapatio"), using a pseudonym
1775	Publishes *The Group*, another satire, this one against the king; she uses a pseudonym
1776	Publishes *The Blockheads*, using a pseudonym
1779	Publishes *The Motley Assembly*, using a pseudonym
1781	The Warrens purchase the estate of Governor Thomas Hutchinson
1788	Wrote *Observations on the New Constitution, and on the Federal and State Convention* using a pseudonym, urging the inclusion of a Bill of Rights and protesting a too-strong central government
1790	Publishes *Poems, Dramatic and Miscellaneous* under her own name. The 18 poems and 2 plays have political themes.
1805	Publishes *History of the Rise, Progress, and Termination of the American Revolution*
1808	Death of James Warren
October 19, 1814	Dies in Plymouth, Massachusetts

Date	Events
November 24, 1943	SS *Mercy Warren*, a Liberty ship, is launched. It was scrapped in 1971.
2002	Voted into the National Women's Hall of Fame (Seneca Falls, New York)

Mercy Otis Warren was an author, poet, playwright, historian and political agitator. She and her husband James Warren were very involved in the Patriot political scene in Massachusetts, and were close associates of John and Abigail Adams, Samuel Adams, Martha Washington and Hannah Winthrop (wife of John Winthrop). The  Committees of Correspondence and the Sons of Liberty used to meet in their home.[133]

Mercy is most famous for her writings, most of which were published anonymously throughout the War. Several of her writings were satires regarding British rule (or misrule) in the colonies. They are reminiscent of some of the writings of Erasmus, such as *Praise of Folly* or *Julius Excluded from Heaven*, during the Protestant Reformation in the 16th century. She wrote several plays, a number of poems, and her brilliant history of the American Revolution. Among her works:

Name	Year	Type of work
The Adulateur	1772 or 1773	Five-act play
The Defeat	1773	Play

---

[133] *Portrait of Mercy Otis Warren* by John Singleton Copley (1738–1815). Public domain.

Name	Year	Type of work
The Group	1775	Three-act play
The Blockheads	1775 or 1776	Three-act play
The Motley Assembly	1779	
Observations on the new Constitution, and on the Federal and State Conventions	1788	Polemic against the proposed Constitution
Poems, Dramatic and Miscellaneous	1790	18 poems and 2 plays
The Rise, Progress and Termination of the American Revolution	1805	3-volume history

Below are three excerpts from her history of the American Revolution. The first gives her reflections on the great victory of the nascent nation against the British, and a look towards the future. It also gives some insight into the lyrical quality of her writing (most of her plays were written in verse):

The young government of this newly established nation had, by the recent articles of peace, a claim to a jurisdiction over a vast territory, reaching from the St. Mary's on the south, to the river St. Croix, the extreme boundary of the east, containing a line of postroads of eighteen hundred miles, exclusive of the northern and western wilds, but partially settled, and whose limits have not yet been explored. Not the Lycian league [now in southern Turkey], nor any of the combinations of the Grecian states, encircled such an extent of territory; nor does modern history furnish any example of a confederacy of equal magnitude and respectability with that of the United States of America.

We look back with astonishment when we reflect, that it was only in the beginning of the seventeenth century, that the first Europeans landed in Virginia, and that nearly at the same time, a few wandering strangers coasted about the unknown bay of Massachusetts, until they found a footing in Plymouth. Only a century and an half had elapsed, before their numbers and their strength accumulated, until they bade defiance to foreign oppression, and stood ready to meet the power of Britain, with courage and magnanimity scarcely paralleled by the progeny of nations, who had been used to every degree of subordination and obedience.

The most vivid imagination cannot realize the contrast, when it surveys the vast surface of America now enrobed with fruitful fields, and the rich herbage of the pastures, which had been so recently covered with a thick mattress of woods; when it beholds the cultivated vista, the orchards and the beautiful gardens which have arisen within the limits of the Atlantic states, where the deep embrowned, melancholy forest, had from time immemorial sheltered only the wandering savage; where the sweet notes of the feathered race, that follow the track of cultivation, had never chanted their melodious songs: the wild waste had been a haunt only for the hoarse birds of prey, and the prowling quadrupeds that filled the forest.

In a country like America, including a vast variety of foil and climate, producing every thing necessary for convenience and pleasure, every man might be lord of his own acquisition. It was a country where the standard of freedom had recently been erected, to allure the liberal minded to her shores, and to receive and to protect the persecuted subjects of arbitrary power, who might there seek an asylum from the chains of servitude to which they had been subjected in any part of the globe. Here it might rationally be expected, that beside the natural increase, the emigrations to a land of such fair promise of the blessings of plenty, liberty, and peace, to which multitudes would probably resort, there would be exhibited in a few years, a population almost beyond the calculation of figures.[134]

Her evaluation of Washington is positive without being fawning, and captures some of the skill he had which are unique to the man.

THE CHARACTER OF WASHINGTON

---

[134] *History of the Rise, Progress, and Termination of the American Revolution*, by Mercy Otis Warren (Manning and Loring, 1805)

Mr. Washington was a gentleman of family and fortune, of a polite, but not a learned education; he appeared to possess a coolness of temper, and a degree of moderation and judgment, that qualified him for the elevated station in which he was now placed; with some considerable knowledge of mankind, he supported the reserve of the statesman, with the occasional affability of the courtier. In his character was blended a certain dignity, united with the appearance of good humour; he possessed courage without rashness, patriotism and zeal without acrimony, and retained with universal applause the first military command, until the establishment of independence. Through the various changes of fortune in the subsequent conflict, though the slowness of his movements was censured by some, his character suffered little diminution to the conclusion of a war, that from the extraordinary exigencies of an infant republic, required at times, the caution of Fabius, the energy of Caesar, and the happy facility of expedient in distress, so remarkable in the military operations of the illustrious Frederick.[135] With the first of these qualities, he was endowed by nature; the second was awakened by necessity; and the third he acquired by experience in the field of glory and danger, which extended his fame through half the globe.

In the late war between England and France, Mr. Washington had been in several military rencounters, and had particularly signalized himself in the unfortunate expedition under general Braddock, in the wilderness on the borders of the Ohio, in the year one thousand seven hundred and fifty-five. His conduct on that occasion raised an eclat of his valor and prudence; in consequence of which many young gentlemen from all parts of the continent, allured by the name of major Washington, voluntarily entered the service, proud of being enrolled in the list of officers under one esteemed so gallant a commander. [136]

Her rather scathing review of Charles Lee was later proved to be spot on. In 1857, a plan for military operations against the colonists written by Lee while a prisoner of the British was found by his descendants.

---

[135] "The late king of Prussia, well known for this trait in his character, by all who are acquainted with the history of his reign."

[136] *History of the Rise, Progress, and Termination of the American Revolution*, by Mercy Otis Warren (Manning and Loring, 1805)

THE CHARACTER OF GENERAL LEE

No man was better qualified at this early stage of the war, to penetrate the designs, or to face in the field an experienced British veteran, than general Lee. He had been an officer of character and rank in the late war between England and France.[137] Fearless of danger, and fond of glory, he was calculated for the field, without any of the graces that recommend the soldier to the circles of the polite. He was plain in his person even to ugliness, and careless in his manners to a degree of rudeness. He possessed a bold genius and an unconquerable spirit: his voice was rough, his garb ordinary, his deportment morose. A considerable traveller, and well acquainted with most of the European nations, he was frequently agreeable in narration, and judicious and entertaining in observation. Disgusted with the ministerial system, and more so with his sovereign who authorized it, he cherished the American cause from motives of resentment, and a predilection in favor of freedom, more than from a just sense of the rights of mankind.

Without religion or country, principle, or attachment, gold was his deity, and liberty the idol of his fancy: he hoarded the former without taste for its enjoyment, and worshipped the latter as the patroness of licentiousness, rather than the protectress of virtue. He affected to despise the opinion of the world, yet was fond of applause. Ambitious of fame without the dignity to support it, he emulated the heroes of antiquity in the field, while in private life he sunk into the vulgarity of the clown. Congress did wisely to avail themselves of his military experience in the infancy of a confederated army, and still more wisely in placing him in a degree of subordination. He was on the first list of continental officers, and only the generals Washington and Ward were named before him; but though nominally the third in rank, as a soldier he was second to no man... nothing remained to prevent this singular stranger from taking the command of the armies of the United States, but the life of Washington.[138]

---

[137] "He had served with reputation in Portugal, under the command of the count de la Lippe."

[138] *History of the Rise, Progress, and Termination of the American Revolution*, by Mercy Otis Warren (Manning and Loring, 1805)

Martha Washington

Date	Events
June 2, 1731	Born Martha Dandridge in New Kent County, Virginia
May 15, 1750	Marries Daniel Parke Custis. They would have four children.
1757	Daniel Parke Custis dies, leaving his widow a fortune
January 6, 1759	Marries George Washington
March 5, 1777	Arrives at the winter encampment in Morristown, New Jersey
February 10, 1778	Arrives at Valley Forge to be with her husband, and quickly becames a popular figure among the troops. She visited the men in their huts, and organized women to knit and sew clothing items for the soldiers.
April 30, 1789	Refuses to attend the inauguration, as she didn't approve of her husband running for president
April 30, 1789 – March 4, 1797	First First Lady of the United States
December 1799	Martha Washington burns almost all letters between her and her husband, after the latter's death
May 22, 1802	Dies in Mount Vernon, Virginia of fever
1860	Martha Washington College opens in Abingdon, Virginia
1886	Appears on the $1 silver certificate
1902	8¢ Martha Washington stamp
1938	1.5¢ Martha Washington stamp
1984	Patty Duke portrays Martha Washington in the TV miniseries *George Washington*
1986	Patty Duke portrays Martha Washington in the TV miniseries *George Washington II: The Forging of a Nation*

Martha Dandridge Custis married George Washington in 1759. At that point, Martha was a wealthy widow – her first husband, Daniel Parke Custis, had died in 1757. Along with Washington's own wealth (some of it granted to him in recognition of his service in the french and Indian War), the couple were quite well-to-do.

Martha Washington[139]

When the Revolutionary War broke out, Martha managed the plantation at Mount Vernon, while Washington was away fighting. However, she would travel (often in inclement weather) to stay with her husband whenever he was in winter encampment, most notably at Valley Forge and at Morristown. She was known for her care for the soldiers, and organizing women to knit and sew clothing items for the soldiers. An idea of her routine at Valley Forge is captured by

[139] Library of Congress http://www.loc.gov/pictures/item/2003688621/

Benson Lossing, we was able to actually interview people who had been with her at Valley Forge.

In all the trials of that winter at Valley Forge, Washington had the most earnest sympathies, cheerful spirit, and willing hands of his loving wife to sustain him and share in his cares. An old lady (Mrs. Westlake) eighty-four years of age, who lived near Mr. Potts's in 1778, with whom I conversed at Norristown more than thirty years ago, said to me,

"I never in my life knew a woman so busy from early morning until late at night as was Lady Washington, providing comforts for the sick soldiers. Every day, excepting Sundays, the wives of officers in camp, and sometimes other women, were invited to Mr. Potts's to assist her in knitting socks, patching garments, and making shirts for the poor soldiers when materials could be procured. Every fair day she might be seen, with basket in hand, and with a single attendant, going among the huts seeking the keenest and most needy sufferers, and giving all the comfort to them in her power. I sometimes went with her, for I was a stout girl, sixteen years old. On one occasion she went to the hut of a dying sergeant, whose young wife was with him. His case seemed to particularly touch the heart of the good lady, and after she had given him some wholesome food she had prepared with her own hands, she knelt down by his straw pallet and prayed earnestly for him and his wife with her sweet and solemn voice. I shall never forget the scene."[140]

An idea of her popularity can be derived from the following account, also from Benson Lossing, of thousands of men cheering Martha and George Washington on the occasion of the Valley Forge encampment celebration of the Colonial alliance with France on May 6, 1778.

The commander-in-chief, with Mrs. Washington, his staff, and Generals Knox and Stirling, with their wives and their aides-de-camp, walked to the head-quarters of Maxwell's New Jersey brigade (not more than half a mile from the army head-quarters), where they were received with a silent military salute from the

---

[140] *Mary and Martha, the Mother and the Wife of George Washington*, by Benson John Lossing (Harper & Brothers, 1886)

soldiery there. They were joined by other officers of the army, with their wives. An appropriate discourse was pronounced by the Rev. Mr. Hunter, after which all the officers of the army present partook of a collation provided by the commander-in-chief, to which two or three Whig families in the neighborhood were invited. When the commander retired, with Mrs. Washington leaning upon his arm, and followed by those who accompanied them from head-quarters, there was a universal huzzaing— "Long live General Washington! Long live Lady Washington!" These demonstrations were continued until the general and his wife had proceeded nearly a quarter of a mile, and a thousand hats were tossed in the air. Washington and his retinue several times returned the huzzas, and the ladies waved their handkerchiefs.[141]

"The reception of Lafayette at Mount Vernon, home of Washington". Martha Washington is on the right.[142]

There are similar accounts of her focus on helping the soldiers at Morristown, as these anecdotes from Charles Hilliard Callahan show:

---

[141] *Mary and Martha, the Mother and the Wife of George Washington*, by Benson John Lossing (Harper & Brothers, 1886)

[142] Library of Congress http://www.loc.gov/pictures/item/2006678648/

Mrs. Washington joined her husband in the New Jersey camp, March 5, 1777, and Dr. Joseph Tuttle gives an amusing account of the experience of some Morristown ladies who paid the General's wife a social call soon after her arrival. "Having a natural desire to appear at their best and to do honor to the great lady, they donned their bravest attire." Mrs. Troupe, one of the party, afterwards relating her experience, says:

We found her knitting and with a speckled apron on. She received us very graciously and easily, but after the compliments were over, she resumed her knitting. There we were without a stitch of work, and sitting in state, while General Washington's lady with her own hands was knitting stockings for herself and husband.

And that was not all. In the afternoon her ladyship took occasion to say, in a way that we could not be offended at, that at this time it was very important that American ladies should be patterns of industry to their countrywomen, because the separation from the mother country will dry up the sources whence many of our comforts have been derived. We must become independent by our determination to do without what we cannot make ourselves. Whilst our husbands and brothers are examples of patriotism, we must be patterns of industry.

Another Morristown woman, in giving an account of the same visit, says:

Yesterday, with several others, I visited Lady Washington at headquarters. We expected to find the wealthy wife of the great general elegantly dressed, for the time of our visit had been fixed; but, instead, she was neatly attired in a plain brown habit. Her gracious and cheerful manners delighted us all, but we felt rebuked by the plainness of her apparel and her example of persistent industry, while we were extravagantly dressed idlers, a name not very creditable in these perilous times. She seems very wise in experience, kind-hearted and winning in all her ways. She talked much of the sufferings of the poor soldiers, especially of the sick ones. Her heart seemed to be full of compassion for them.[143]

---

[143] *Washington: The Man and the Mason*, by Charles Hilliard Callahan (Memorial Temple Committee of the George Washington Masonic National Memorial Association, 1915)

Martha Washington, whose devotion to her husband and the Colonial cause never wavered, is included here as a heroine of the Revolution because of her undying devotion to the common soldier.

Sources

- *A Colored Man's Reminiscences of James Madison*, by Paul Jennings (George C. Beadle, 1865)
- *A Narrative of Some of the Adventures, Dangers and Sufferings of a Revolutionary Soldier*, by Joseph Plumb Martin (Glazier, Masters & Co., 1830)
- *A Short History of Molly Pitcher, the Heroine of the Battle of Monmouth*, by John B. Landis (The Cornman Printing Company, 1905)
- *Alexander Hamilton's Famous Report on Manufactures: Made to Congress In His Capacity as Secretary of the Treasury*, by Alexander Hamilton (Home Market Club, 1892)
- *Brief Sketch of the Life of Thomas Paine*, (Solomon King, 1830)
- *Colonel Henry Ludington: A Memoir*, by Willis Fletcher Johnson (Lavinia Elizabeth Ludington and Charles Henry Ludington, 1907)
- *Dakota Farmers' Leader*, (Canton, S.D.), July 3, 1896
- *Deseret Evening News*, (Deseret, Utah) July 16, 1910
- *Ethan Allen's Narrative of the Capture of Ticonderoga: And of His Captivity and Treatment by the British*, by Ethan Allen (C. Goodrich & S. B. Nichols, 1849)
- *General Orders of Geo. Washington: Issued at Newburgh 1782-1783*, compiled by Edward C. Boynton (E. N. Ruttenbur, 1883)
- *Hesperian, Volume 2, The*, by William Davis Gallagher, Otway Curry (John D. Nichols, 1838)
- *History of the Flag of the United States*, by William Canby; A Paper read before the Historical Society of Pennsylvania, The (March 1870)
- *History of the Rise, Progress, and Termination of the American Revolution*, by Mercy Otis Warren (Manning and Loring, 1805)
- *John Hancock: His Book*, by Abram English Brown (Lee and Shepard Publishers, 1898)
- *Letter from Alexander Hamilton, Concerning the Public Conduct and Character of John Adams, Esq. President Of The United States*, by Alexander Hamilton (Printed for John Lang by George F. Hopkins, 1800)
- *Letters and Other Writings of James Madison: 1769-1793*, by James Madison (J.B. Lippincott & Co., 1865)

- *Letters of Mrs. Adams: The Wife of John Adams*, by Abigail Adams, John Quincy Adams, Charles Francis Adams (Wilkins, Carter and Co., 1848)
- *Life and Correspondence of John Paul Jones*, by John Paul Jones, Janette Taylor (A. Chandler, 1830)
- *Life of Esther De Berdt: Afterwards Esther Reed, of Pennsylvania, The*, by William Bradford Reed(C. Sherman, printer, 1853)
- *Life of Francis Marion, The*, by William Gilmore Simm (George F. Cooledge & Brother, 1813)
- *Life of General Daniel Morgan, The*, by James Graham (Derby & Jackson, 1856)
- *Life of General Francis Marion, The*, by Mason Locke Weems, Peter Horry (J. B. Lippincott, 1860)
- *Lydia Darragh, One of the Heroines of the Revolution*, by Henry Darrach (City History Society of Philadelphia, 1916)
- *Magazine of American History with Notes and Queries, Volume 16, The*, by Martha Joanna Lamb (Historical Publication Company, 1886)
- *Mary and Martha, the Mother and the Wife of George Washington*, by Benson John Lossing (Harper & Brothers, 1886)
- *Nathanael Greene*, by George Washington Greene (Tichnor and Fields, 1866)
- *Official Letters to the Honorable American Congress*, by George Washington (Cadell, Junior and Davies, 1795)
- *Perrysburg Journal*, (Perrysburg, Wood Co., O. [Ohio]), March 16, 1906
- *Pullman Herald*, (Pullman, W.T. [Wash.]), July 5, 1902
- *Putnam County Courier*, (Carmel, N.Y.), June 30, 1960
- *Romance of the Revolution, The*, by Oliver Bell Bunce (Porter & Coates, 1870)
- *Salt Lake Tribune*, August 21, 1910
- *Sketches of the Life and Character of Patrick Henry*, by William Wirt (Claxton, Kemsen & Haffelfinger, 1832)
- *Steuben's Regulations for the Order and Discipline of the Troops of the United States*, by Friedrich Wilhelm Ludolf Gerhard Augustin Baron von Steuben (Printed for William Pelham, 1807)
- *Washington: The Man and the Mason*, by Charles Hilliard Callahan (Memorial Temple Committee of the George Washington Masonic National Memorial Association, 1915)
- *Women of the American Revolution, Volume 1, The*, by Elizabeth Fries Ellet (Baker and Scribner, 1819)

- *Works of Alexander Hamilton, The*, by Alexander Hamilton (John F. Trow, 1850)
- *Writings of Samuel Adams: 1773-1777, Volume III, The*, by Samuel Adams (G. P. Putnam's Sons, 1907)

Links

http://avalon.law.yale.edu/18th_century/washing.asp
http://en.wikipedia.org/wiki/List_of_places_named_for_Francis_Marion
http://www-personal.umd.umich.edu/~ppennock/doc-Sentiments%20of%20An
%20American%20Woman.htm
http://www.archives.gov/exhibits/charters/declaration_transcript.html
http://www.archives.gov/research/military/american-
http://www.bartleby.com/124/pres15.html
http://www.constitution.org/jadams/thoughts.htm
http://www.gpo.gov/fdsys/pkg/STATUTE-90/pdf/STATUTE-90-Pg2078.pdf
http://www.gutenberg.org/files/20203/20203-h/20203-h.htm#XVIII
http://www.gutenberg.org/files/45205/45205-h/45205-h.htm
http://www.historicphiladelphia.org/betsy-ross-house/history/
http://www.law.ou.edu/ushistory/henry.shtml
http://www.loc.gov/pictures/item/91792202/
http://www.masshist.org/database/99
http://www.ushistory.org/betsy/more/canby.htm
Library of Congress   http://www.loc.gov/pictures/item/2007681477/
Library of Congress   http://www.loc.gov/pictures/item/2009633684/
Library of Congress   http://hdl.loc.gov/loc.gmd/g3804t.ar117500
Library of Congress   http://www.loc.gov/loc/lcib/0307-8/hale.html
Library of Congress   http://www.loc.gov/pictures/item/2002707681/
Library of Congress   http://www.loc.gov/pictures/item/2002719535/
Library of Congress   http://www.loc.gov/pictures/item/2002725153/
Library of Congress   http://www.loc.gov/pictures/item/2003663990/
Library of Congress   http://www.loc.gov/pictures/item/2003671510/
Library of Congress   http://www.loc.gov/pictures/item/2003679975/
Library of Congress   http://www.loc.gov/pictures/item/2003688621/
Library of Congress   http://www.loc.gov/pictures/item/2003689054/
Library of Congress   http://www.loc.gov/pictures/item/2006676692/
Library of Congress   http://www.loc.gov/pictures/item/2006678648/
Library of Congress   http://www.loc.gov/pictures/item/2006691555/
Library of Congress   http://www.loc.gov/pictures/item/2006691580/
Library of Congress   http://www.loc.gov/pictures/item/2006691581/
Library of Congress   http://www.loc.gov/pictures/item/2008661777/
Library of Congress   http://www.loc.gov/pictures/item/2008676310/
Library of Congress   http://www.loc.gov/pictures/item/2009631979/
Library of Congress   http://www.loc.gov/pictures/item/2010720200/
Library of Congress   http://www.loc.gov/pictures/item/2012645366/
Library of Congress   http://www.loc.gov/pictures/item/2012645953/
Library of Congress   http://www.loc.gov/pictures/item/2014637201/

Robert is available as a speaker. See
http://rcjbooks.com/guest_speaker for details.

Front cover:

George Washington, by Charles Willson Peale, 1776
Public domain. The White House Historical Association.

Portrait of Paul Revere by John Singleton Copley
Public domain. Museum of Fine Arts Boston.

"The women of '76: "Molly Pitcher" the heroine of Monmouth"
Library of Congress http://www.loc.gov/pictures/item/2002698846/

About the Author

Robert C. Jones is President of the Kennesaw Historical Society, and is a member of the Executive Board of the Kennesaw Museum Foundation. He has written several books on Civil War, Revolutionary War and railroad themes, including:

- *A Guide to the Civil War in Georgia*
- *Battle of Allatoona Pass: The Forgotten Battle of Sherman's Atlanta Campaign, The*
- *Battle of Chickamauga: A Brief History, The*
- *Battle of Griswoldville: An Infantry Battle on Sherman's March to the Sea, The*
- *Bleeding Kansas: The Real Start of the Civil War*
- *Civil War Prison Camps: A Brief History*
- *Confederate Invasion of New Mexico, The*
- *Conspirators, Assassins, and the Death of Abraham Lincoln*
- *The End of the Civil War in Georgia: 1865*
- *Famous Songs of the Civil War*
- *Fifteen Most Critical Moments of the Civil War, The*
- *George Washington and the Continental Army: 1777/1778*
- *Great Naval Battles of the Civil War*
- *Heroes and Heroines of the American Revolution*
- *McCook's Raid and the Battle of Brown's Mill*
- *Pennsylvania Railroad: An Illustrated Timeline, The*
- *Reading Railroad: An Illustrated Timeline, The*
- *Retracing the Route of Sherman's Atlanta Campaign (expanded edition)*
- *Retracing the Route of Sherman's March to the Sea (expanded edition)*
- *Top 10 Reasons Why the Civil War Was Won in the West, The*
- *Ten Best – and Worst – Generals of the Civil War, The*
- *Top 20 Civil War Spies and Secret Agents, The*
- *Top 20 Railroad Songs of All Time, The*
- *Top 25 Most Influential Women of the Civil War, The*
- *W&A, the General, and the Andrews Raid: A Brief History, The*

Robert is an ordained elder in the Presbyterian Church. He has written and taught numerous adult Sunday School courses. He is also the author of a number of books on Christian history and theology topics. For a list, see http://rcjbooks.com/christian_history.

Robert has also written several books on "Old West" themes, including:

- *Death Valley Ghost Towns – As They Appear Today*
- *Ghost Towns, Forts and Pueblos of New Mexico* (expanded edition)
- *Ghost Towns of Southern Arizona and New Mexico*
- *Ghost Towns of the Mojave National Preserve*
- *Ghost Towns of Western Nevada*
- *Top 10 Gunslingers and Lawmen of the Old West, The*

In 2005, Robert co-authored a business-oriented book entitled *Working Virtually: The Challenges of Virtual Teams*.

In 2013, Robert authored a book on World War I, entitled *The Top 10 Innovations of World War I*.

Also in 2013, Robert published *The Leo Beuerman Story: As Told by his Family*.

In 2014, Robert published *Ghost Towns and Mills of the Atlanta Area*.

http://www.rcjbooks.com/
jone442@bellsouth.net

Made in the USA
Columbia, SC
24 February 2021